D1597307

ANGEL WITH A BUSHY BEARD

DUDLEY GARDINER

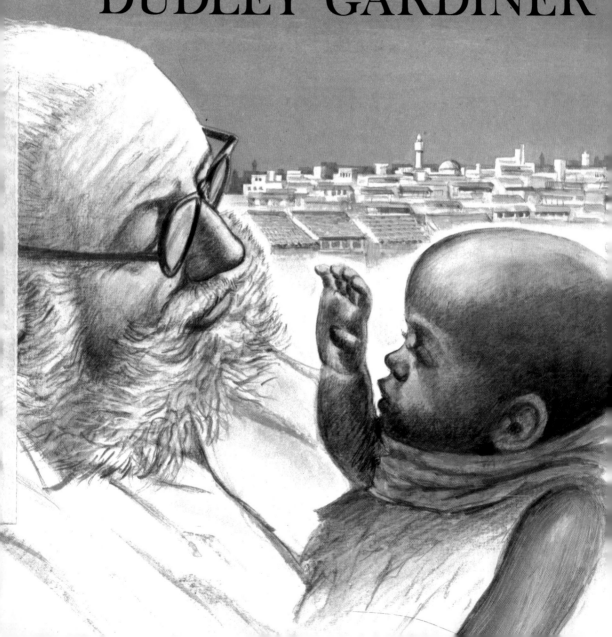

Angel
with a
Bushy Beard

Angel
with a
Bushy Beard

DUDLEY GARDINER MBE

THE SAINT ANDREW PRESS

EDINBURGH

First published in 1980 by
THE SAINT ANDREW PRESS
121 George Street, Edinburgh EH2 4YN

Copyright © DUDLEY GARDINER 1980
ISBN 0 7152 0425 4

Printed by McCorquodale (Scotland) Ltd, 96 Maxwell Street, Glasgow

H V 28
.G27 A32
1980 **Contents**
GETS

Erratum

The publishers regret the error in captions to the photographs on pages 75 and 80. The photograph on page 75 is of Commissioner Don Smith, and on page 80 of Captain Robert Bath.

Acknowledgements

The publishers thank the following organisations for the use of photographic material: Camera Press, London (Arun Ganguly, photographer)—pages 86, 88, 97, 107, 109 (lower right), 110, 114, 116; Christian Aid, Information Unit, London—pages 87, 89; Church of Our Lady of the Wayside, Shirley, Solihull—pages 85, 105, 109 (lower left), 113; Help the Aged, Press Office, London—page 109 (top); Imperial War Museum, London—pages 8, 10, 16, 20, 28, 31, 32, 33, 36, 38, 41, 42, 43, 44, 46, 48, 55; Salvation Army, Information Services, London—pages 59, 75 (upper left), 75 (lower), 76, 77, 78, 79 (upper and lower), 80, 81, 83, 91, 100 (upper and lower), 101 (upper and lower), 106, 121, 122.

Preface

Calcutta assaults the senses and it also assaults the mind. It is a city of vivid and frightening contrasts. It is pulsating with life and yet death seems to hover over the city like the fetid blanket of heat over square miles of decaying buildings. It is a city of wealth, rich trading, prosperous businessmen. But it is also a city of hopelessness for hundreds of thousands who live in the bustees— poorly constructed shacks packed tightly together with no sanitation, each one housing an entire family. Of all the cities in India, Calcutta has the greatest social consciousness, and yet it cannot even begin to solve the problems on its own doorstep.

Most Europeans living in Calcutta manage to survive by shutting out the unpleasant and shocking aspects of the city. They live in a cosy cocoon of unreality consisting of pleasant houses, air-conditioned offices, clubs and cocktail parties. Any European who is going to try to come to grips with some of Calcutta's social problems requires to be someone out of the ordinary. And a European who is actually going to *work* with the destitutes of the city needs to have a commitment way beyond the normal missionary zeal and ideal of service.

Calcutta has two such people. Mother Teresa is well known. Her extra-ordinary service to suffering humanity in Calcutta and elsewhere has rightly caught the world's attention.

This book is the story, told simply by himself, of the other 'saint' of Calcutta—Dudley Gardiner. A near neighbour of Mother Teresa's, his work in the city is practical, unglamorous and monotonous. Each day he makes sure that over seven thousand men, women and children receive one good meal, without which they would probably starve or be reduced to begging or stealing. This work is carried out at a sacrificial cost to himself which is humbling to all who know him.

A rather lonely, isolated childhood, followed by a career in the army, fostered the self-discipline and tough mental attitude necessary for the rigorous life he later chose. His experiences on the North West Frontier of India and, later, in Burma (he was taken prisoner by the Japanese and was one of those forced to work on the infamous Burma-Siam Railway) led him to think deeply about life and its meaning.

When he retired from the army, having reached the rank of Major, he made a decision with all the sincerity and solemnity of a monk taking holy orders. He would devote the remainder of his life to helping suffering humanity. He made up his mind that this commitment would be complete and unswerving— and he has been true to his word. He has sacrificed comfort and the material things of life, marriage, the warmth of companionship and friendship, so that his commitment could be total.

Dudley Gardiner claims that all through his life he has been searching for God. God, surely, found *him* a long time ago. Unquestionably his physical strength despite constant illness and discomfort, and his mental strength despite loneliness and bouts of depression, are God-given. By his example of dedication and service he has surely given a positive answer to that most difficult of questions in the New Testament: 'Who is my neighbour?' His answer is, uncompromisingly: 'Everyone.'

Dudley Gardiner is known as the 'angel with a bushy beard'. To anyone who has met him, the impact of his personality and the scope yet sheer monotony of his work will never be forgotten. It is the hope of the publishers that, as he tells his own story, that impact will be felt through the pages of this book.

1 A Soldier's Son

In my own way I have tried during the last twenty years of my life here in the slums of Calcutta, which is perhaps one of the most depressed areas in the world, to answer with compassion the crying needs of Calcutta's flotsam.

My dear friend and source of inspiration, Mother Teresa, has at the centre of her dynamic work a complete and utter belief in God. Her burning faith is simple, uncluttered by theological nuances. She loves and trusts God and he has used her to accomplish miracles in Calcutta, where one might be tempted to think that with so much poverty God had closed his eyes to human suffering and human dereliction. To her, all the inhabitants of Calcutta are God's children, all precious in his sight, all to be loved regardless of their condition and, remarkably, regardless of their religion.

Why have I started an account of my life by paying tribute to a plain little nun who bullies me? She is a mere five feet

and I am six feet two inches and twenty stones in weight and yes, she bullies me. Not unkindly, I hasten to add, but when she wants something badly, she insists, and one feels that one is also arguing with God himself. It is an unequal struggle from the start! I always capitulate—but find joy in seeing her creased face clear into the smile that has opened shut doors, opened closed purses, and has softened hearts as hard as flint. Why then do I mention her? Mother Teresa's name and need in Calcutta are synonymous. Her work is known and admired worldwide. She has travelled extensively and the aura of unworldliness which she carries with her always has had a profound effect on all who meet her. She has a Ghandian simplicity—a directness, which in a world used to deviousness is as refreshing as the first monsoon rains on the parched plains of India.

I have no such charisma. I could not compete in a popularity poll against

Mother Teresa. I would be a non-starter. The work I do in Calcutta is non-imaginative compared to the outreach of Mother Teresa into various areas of need. My work has not changed all that much in twenty years. Twenty years ago I came to Calcutta and decided that the greatest need for the thousands of jobless pavement-dwellers and destitutes was food. My goal was to feed as many of them daily as I could. It was a simple goal. Perhaps my one claim to some kind of pat on the back is that I have not deviated for even one day from that simple goal. It has not been easy. You see Mother Teresa always has God to help her with her planning—God to discuss her triumphs and to share her disappointments. God to me is very real, don't mistake me, but I have never honestly felt the close personal relationship which Mother Teresa enjoys. As a result, I have lived a lonely life, almost a solitary life, almost monastic in its following of a rigid schedule. It has left no time for pleasure, no time for gracious living. Often in my solitary room at night, I feel as if I am trapped by circumstances.

As I grow older and perhaps a little less active I feel as if I am caught in a never ending merry-go-round, trapped by my feeling of responsibility to the hungry thousands I feed daily. I often long for the company of a woman—a softening influence for my life. The sexual fires have long gone out; I simply crave companionship. I would be a difficult, impossible person to live with. I am as conditioned to my bizarre life in Calcutta as Pavlov's dogs were conditioned to their

bells. For twenty years I have followed the same monotonous round day in and day out. Why? I think, if I am honest, I, as an ordinary man with no pretension of cleverness, or with any special talents, like the feeling that thousands of people depend on me—depend on me for existence. It gives me a warm feeling—a feeling of well-being. The smile from an old woman, dying of tuberculosis, as I give her a cup of rice makes all the dull monotony of my life bearable. I feel that twenty years ago I accepted a challenge—that of doing something practical about desperate need and in some ways it has become an obsession. It has devoured me, but I have faithfully, in sickness and in health, been true to the hungry to whom I minister. In a way I feel I have been true to myself.

I have led a solitary life. If I had not, I would not have been able to cope with the confining life I now lead. My life has been rich in experience, but poor in meaningful relationships. I have had hosts of acquaintances and few friends.

I suppose all influences which touch us as we journey through life add something to our personalities. My life has been largely played out in India. Anyone who knows India well, realises that you either love India with all the passion one is capable of, or you absolutely detest it. There is no middle course. One can never be indifferent to India. It makes claims on the emotions like no other country I know. Even Calcutta—ugly, sprawling, depressing Calcutta, which assaults the senses, with its noise, its smells, its chaotic disorder, its grinding poverty has claimed my heart, and I have no desire to leave it. I have not been in England for twenty years and I have no desire to see the inevitable changes which have occurred in that time, I would rather remember the England of my younger days—an idealised England—a green England, an ordered England, an England of Wimbledon, Lord's and Henley. Often at night in my plain, scrubbed room in Lower Circular Road, Calcutta, my mind, as happens with elderly people, dwells on the past, on my childhood and the beginnings of young Dudley Gardiner, set in an England in the pre-First World War period. It is strange how old age accentuates sentimentality. It is odd too the strange tricks that memory can play. To put my recollections down on paper I have dredged into the recesses of my mind. By doing this, I have been conscious of landmarks in my life, influences which helped to mould me and, at twenty stones, it requires to be a rather large mould!

I live in Calcutta in quarters provided by the Salvation Army, an organisation for which I have the highest possible regard. Knowing the views of the good folk in the Salvation Army on alcohol I like to shock them by informing them that I was born in a pub or, to be more accurate, above a pub in 1910. I might add I was a bit choosey about the pub I was born above. It was a very well-known one in those far off days and it is, I gather, very well known and popular today. It is called the Roebuck Hotel, and is situated at the top of Richmond Hill.

The hotel commands a magnificent view of the sweep of the Thames down towards Hampton Court. I gather that just across the road from the hotel is a specially constructed viewing platform where the various well-known landmarks on the Thames are shown. At this viewpoint there is recorded the fact that in the early eighteenth century William Byrd, seeing the view, was reminded of a similar view on the James River, Virginia, and this inspired him to name the new town which was to be created on that site, Richmond, Virginia. Anyway I chose a select pub with a splendid view, to be born in.

My parents married when they were very young. My mother was only seventeen when I was born. Her maiden name was Catherine Ann Sauvary and she was of French extraction. My father was a regular soldier in the Royal Fusiliers. I was to follow him in that profession and between us we were to complete sixty-four years of service, most of it in India.

The barracks occupied by the Royal Fusiliers in Hounslow, Middlesex, were pretty dilapidated and uninviting. A private soldier's pay was a pittance and my parents found it practically impossible to make ends meet. My mother, who was neat and pretty, found a job as a barmaid in the Roebuck Hotel. In those distant days to be a barmaid was highly suspect, but this particular hotel had a very special reputation, and so to be a barmaid at the Roebuck did not carry the same stigma that being a barmaid in other pubs did. I think she was probably very efficient at her job. The reason I say

The Roebuck Hotel, Richmond, Surrey, England—birthplace of Dudley Gardiner

View of the River Thames from the Roebuck

this is because when the time came for me to see the light of day, the owner of the hotel suggested that rather than go back to the ramshackle barracks to have her confinement she should just go upstairs have the baby and, when she felt fit and the baby was fine, she could return to the bar!

Unfortunately my birth was not an easy one, and it was not possible for my mother, young as she was, to have any more children. This fact was an influence on my life. It meant a certain isolation, for being a soldier's son meant constant moves to new environments and I was frequently having to adapt not only to new surroundings, but new playmates and companions. I don't think I was very good at this.

My early memories of the Roebuck Hotel are happy ones. My parents were young and happy and laughed a lot. The Roebuck attracted a fascinating cross-section of customers. It was a well-known theatrical haunt and its best known patron was Sir John Martin Harvey. I have a vivid memory of this larger-than-life actor. His very talk was theatrical. He believed in the grand gestures. He treated the patrons of the Roebuck to a performance every time he came in, usually a Sunday morning as I remember. He dressed in flamboyant style: purple cravat, a big black floppy hat, a long morning coat, and cane and cigar. He would bend down and pat me on the head and say something pleasant to me. Lady Helen Terry also used to come to the Roebuck. I must have been about four at the time. The memory of these theatrical

stars is really my first vivid memory.

We were very isolated as a family. Sadly, we saw little of our relatives because religion caused a division in the family. My father was a Protestant and my mother a Roman Catholic and both families found it difficult to reconcile this fact. My mother eventually turned Protestant, but even this big step did not reconcile her to my father's family. I rarely heard my parents talk of my grandparents. The result was that the three of us were very much alone.

Perhaps as a result of this sad situation I detest religious bigotry of any kind. After all, the faith that we have is really an accident of birth, and we generally become indoctrinated in the faith of our parents. This is a fact which is often conveniently forgotten. As I grow older I have learnt more and more to respect the faith of others. World religions have grown out of the mythology and the culture of the people and, no matter what their form of religion, most people are groping for the truth, searching for purpose and meaning in life. The method of the search varies but usually leads to an unseen power which is worshipped by all religions with awe and wonder.

My mother's spinal disease left her very crippled and to a certain extent very dependent on my father. She always walked with a stick. Looking back he must have been quite mature to cope with a crippled wife and a child on a pittance.

I wish I could say that my father was always kind to my mother. Sadly this was not the case. He could be very impatient with her and scold her quite severely. I remember being quite upset and feeling helpless, and I would cry and hope that my father would be kind to her. On the whole, however, I think they were reasonably happy together and I think my father was really quite devoted to her. He certainly took her everywhere with him on all his postings whilst some soldiers left their wives behind.

I vividly remember my mother's grief when my father went to France in 1914. She cried, and for some reason which I cannot fathom he got very angry with her tears. I remember him shouting at her and stuffing a handkerchief in her mouth to stop her crying. Perhaps he was afraid. He was very young and the casualty lists coming from France and Belgium were long and frightening.

My mother and I stayed in barracks which were austere and cold. My mother went to work in a pub and I attended a council school in Middlesex. I remember little of this school. It made little impression on me. My mother and I led very restricted lives. She collected me from school at night and we never went out much. Then in 1918, when the war was over, my father returned. He was one of the lucky ones; he had miraculously survived four years of trench warfare. My memory of the War is confined to one horrifying sight. One day I was looking out of the back window of our barrack room, when down the road came a great number of horse-drawn ambulances. The ambulances were open and I could see that they were full of wounded soldiers with blood-soaked bandages round their heads and arms. They had just come off a ship from France, and I remember looking anxiously to see if my father was amongst them. From that day on, I remember being afraid that I would never see him again.

The day he came home was an exciting one. This time my father did not get angry at my mother's tears. He was a fine looking figure in khaki. He was tall and straight and I remember the feel and the smell of his khaki uniform. He was a hero in my eyes. I think from that moment I made up my mind that I wanted to be a soldier like him. I think in all fairness it should be said that my father had probably already come to the same conclusion! In those days it was thought fitting and right for sons of soldiers to enter the boys' service, much the same way I suppose that miners' sons went down the pits like their fathers. Anyway, the decision that I should become a soldier was mutually agreed and my military career started (would you believe?) at the tender age of eight.

I was sent to a military school in Somerset and I was rather frightened to be leaving home, but in some ways I was glad to escape the continual bickering and squabbling which constantly went on at home. My mother's health was poor and made her waspish. Four years in the trenches had changed my father. He always had a hot temper and his experiences had obviously not helped this weakness. His health too in damp England was never very good at this time. So I was quite glad to leave the tensions and I thoroughly enjoyed the four years I spent at this school, which was beautifully sited at Shepton Mallet near the Somerset

Boys at a military school

coast. I loved the sea, in summer and winter, and I liked nothing better than walking on the cliffs and dreaming my dreams.

It was good to be with boys my own age. Our school routine was rigid, but I enjoyed its security. I have always been amenable to fair discipline and in these early days of my career in the military school in the West Country I was broken in, as it were. Like all the other boys I accepted it as a training not only for being a soldier but as a training for manhood. I suppose we were old beyond our years. We played at being soldiers, when other boys of our age were playing with toys and games. We perhaps missed a stage in our natural development. We were taught to think as soldiers, to act as soldiers. We were taught that to fight and die for King and country, as millions had so recently done, was the greatest honour that could befall us. This was constantly stressed, probably to counter the inevitable public reaction to the holocaust which had just ended. Although Europe was at peace there were still turbulent areas in the Empire which required to be policed and protected. Anyway, I know I accepted the discipline and in fact I liked it. I like order, tidiness and punctuality, so I took to the régime like a duck takes to water and would have happily continued at the school if my father had not obtained a posting to India.

The news of his posting was received by my parents with mixed feelings. How would my mother's condition react to the heat of India? My father, I think, was quite excited at the prospect of soldiering in a new environment. The North West Frontier was full of tensions and the stories circulating in the army about the Pathans and their feats round the Khyber Pass rivalled the romantic stories of the Foreign Legion and their skirmishes with the tribesmen in the Sahara.

The voyage out to India by troopship was a bit of a nightmare. As I mentioned, I love the sea and my heart leapt when I saw the troopship and looked forward to the weeks I would spend on board. I had not realised that the army, like society in England at that time, had a very rigid social structure. On the troopship were officers and their ladies, warrant officers, NCO's and their wives, soldiers and their women. Yes, three categories: ladies, wives and women! My father was not an NCO and my mother was one of the women, so our quarters on the trooper were right down below the waterline where the toilets were. We were hopelessly overcrowded and as we sailed down the Red Sea towards Aden the heat was unbearable. The voyage seemed interminable.

We stopped at various places like Suez and Aden but we were never allowed ashore. We were allowed to stand only on a certain area of the deck. It was frustrating in the extreme not to be allowed ashore in these very foreign and exotic-looking places. We were not allowed on the top deck at all as it was reserved for officers and their families. I remember spending a lot of time just looking out of portholes and wishing that India would heave into sight when we would be able to leave the cramped

HM Transport Ship Dunera

quarters and I would be able to run about on land again.

There seemed to be hundreds of children on board and occasionally classes were arranged for us. As far as I remember there was little arranged in the way of entertainment for the children. We were treated as some kind of encumbrance.

We sailed at the end of the year, the then migrating period for the military. Troopships usually arrived in India between the months of October and February, the cool season in the sub-continent, so that newcomers could acclimatise better.

At last we dropped anchor off Bombay and I had my first look at the country which was to exasperate and yet enthrall me. Little did I realise that day in January 1922 that I was destined to spend a very large proportion of my life amongst the teeming millions of this fascinating country.

After the cramped quarters almost in the bilges of the trooper, the Gateway of India looked very welcoming indeed. As we landed from the lighter we seemed to be swamped by a deluge of humanity— the persistent sweating coolies descended on our luggage like locusts. My impression that day was of heat, flies and a memory of graceful palm trees bordering the avenues as we were transported by truck to a camp called Kalabar up on the heights overlooking Bombay. Down at the dockyard a funny thing happened before we entered the camp. I was twelve years old and big for my age. The school in Somerset had smartened me up and I was

well-built and muscular. The soldiers in the camp lined me up with the rest of the draft and issued me with two bed sheets, a Bakelite case to put soap in and a packet of cigarettes. I gave the cigarettes to my father, kept the plastic box, and slept between sheets for the first time in my life!

The camp was quite a pleasant one, but the heat was hard to take to begin with. One good result of the heat was that my mother's physical condition improved with the warmth. With cheap servants available to help with the cooking and the housework, the lot of even the privates' 'women' was a very pleasant one.

I remember the fascination of my visits to the Crawford Market and walking along the dramatic sweep of Marine Drive. It was like something out of the Arabian Nights—the colour, the move-ment, the bargaining, the delicious spicy smells from food stalls and, above all, the fun of driving through the packed, throbbing streets in a *gharry*—a horse-drawn cab. Being an only child I had quite an imagination and I found living in Bombay at an impressionable age stimulating and exciting.

Bombay at this time, however, was deceptive. The National Congress Party were beginning to make their considerable influence felt. Mahatma Gandhi had caught the public's imagination, the non-violence campaigns had started and Bombay city had been affected by it early on. Bombay was one of the strongholds of the Congress at this time. It was very political. The troops, including my father, were constantly on duty in the city dealing with civil disorders, and trying to prevent mobs gathering. I remember there were troops on guard at most of the street corners in the centre of the city, some of them actually carrying dummy guns made of wood. Why they did this, goodness knows! It could be very tense indeed as not all the Congress followers were committed to non-violence.

I had strict instructions never to go out alone in the city. I had either to go with my parents, or other soldiers. My great friend was the army postman and one day, just after we arrived in Bombay, I accompanied him to the Post Office in the city to collect the sea mail which had just arrived. I distinctly remember getting out of the old ramshackle van and walking along a street which seemed to be covered with blood, and all up the steps of the Post Office were patches of blood, and all over the walls and floor in the Post Office the same liberal sprinkling of blood. I could not get back to camp quickly enough. I did not want to show the postman, who seemed to be very brave, that I was frightened. On returning to the Camp I told my father what happened. 'Listen', I said, 'I do not want to visit the Post Office again as there was blood all over the place'. My father looked startled and went to speak to the postman. He came back roaring with laughter. 'Your blood was betel nut pan', he said, and went on to explain that Indians chew this nut and spit out the red juice. In fact, when I became a soldier I used to chew it myself. It is a great aid to digestion, but I'm afraid I've gone off it now.

After some weeks in Bombay in the transit camp, my father's posting to Jabbalpur came through. I went with them and their home was a bell-tent. It was divided in half by a *purdah*, a cloth screen, and half was bedroom and the other half living quarters. We had no *punkas* (fans) and no electricity. There were plenty of ants and creepy-crawly creatures, however.

I was sent from Jabbalpur by train in the company of a post clerk to Lovedale Military Academy in South India. I lived in luxury at Lovedale and I loved it. The school was in the Nilgri Hills and enjoyed a very pleasant climate.

At Lovedale there were about four hundred and fifty boys. I was delighted to be back in the boarding school situation. I always preferred the order and stability of the boarding school life to the tensions and strife of home. My mother was not anxious for me to leave Jabbalpur, but I think my father was really quite glad to see the departure of the big hulking lad who took up a lot of room in the tent, apart from anything else! My mother was not too well again and all in all I was quite glad to leave Jabbalpur for the South.

My time at Lovedale was one of the happiest of my life. The boys there were all the sons of officers and men and we were rather subtly segregated. We were in different dormitories, without this being made obvious. It 'just happened' that all of the officers' sons would be placed in different dormitories from the sons of the other ranks. The officers' sons had better clothes and uniforms and much more pocket money. The education and training, however, were common to all students.

I had khaki shorts and shirt and a helmet with a bandeau round it, puttees, boots and gaiters and my own rifle which was kept locked in a cupboard in the dormitory when I was not carrying it. For thirty-six years I was to wear this uniform.

The dormitories were spotlessly clean and airy and the food was superb as it was suited to the tastes of officers' sons. The only resentment I felt about the segregation was the fact that there was such a difference in the amount of pocket money!

We followed a very tough curriculum. Our headmaster was a scholarly man and was adamant that the boys should have a good education as well as training in the military skills. The staff consisted of well-trained military officers from England on contract to teach military tactics, history, and field craft to the boys, and there were also trained teachers, including lecturers from Cardiff University, who came on a three-year contract to teach 'the 3 Rs' and broaden our education. There were constant battles between the military teachers and the boffins (as we called the non-military teachers). The headmaster unashamedly favoured the boffins. He thought, I think correctly, that there would be ample time for us to learn the art of war when we entered full military service. The military teachers were always spick and span while very often the boffins were untidy and one or two of them had their trousers kept up by bits of string.

The whole atmosphere was very *pucka*.

The school could have been situated in the middle of rural England for all the contact we had with the Indian environment. We were, for example, not allowed to eat Indian sweets and all our sweets were brought out from England by ship in bottles: brandy balls, liquorice all-sorts, palm toffees; never were we allowed to eat anything that was not cooked in the Academy cookhouse. I loved rice and Indian food, but all the time I was at Lovedale I was fed on good, solid English cooking.

Needless to say some of us had cultivated a taste for Indian sweetmeats and so we used to climb over the wall and purchase sweets from the local Bazaar and on our return hide the spoils of our raid in our tuck-boxes. To be caught at this, as I frequently was, meant three or four weeks confined to the school and deprived of all sport and outings. This quite severe punishment did not deter us from our trips over the wall! There was a delicious sense of adventure in evading detection, and a real feeling of accomplishment when the sweets were safely stowed away in the tuck-box—not to mention the delight of filling ourselves with the very sickly sweetness of the Indian delicacies.

I enjoyed Lovedale immensely. I remember receiving a letter from my father saying he was coming from Jabbalpur to pay me a visit. This was most unusual and I wondered what his visit was all about. It transpired that he had been posted back to the United Kingdom for three years and then he would return to India; he had come to ask me if I wished to return to the UK with them or stay on at Lovedale. I recall making the spontaneous decision, from which I never wavered, that I would stay on at Lovedale. Looking back, I suppose it was rather an odd choice. I think part of my decision was caused by the fact that they were returning to Hounslow Barracks and I had rather unhappy memories of the bleak three-apartment quarters we had in the tenement-like barracks. Compared to the life of luxury I was leading at Lovedale, Hounslow had all the appeal of a prison. My father accepted my decision, came down to see me once before they sailed to the UK and promised to write to me regularly. He did write to me, but mail came by sea in those days and letters could take up to three months to arrive. This did not worry me for I was really very independent by this time. I did not miss my parents unduly and I do not think they pined for me, because they did not come rushing to see me when they returned to India. In fact they had been back about four months before I went up to join them for a holiday in Jabbalpur. This holiday was not a great success. It was the hot season and there were no fans in the tent and the food was not really up to Lovedale's standards, and I was really quite delighted when it was time to return to school. I think my mother was glad to see me. She was really quite proud that I had grown so big and strong.

2 On The North West Frontier

My time at Lovedale eventually finished and it was with genuine regret that I left at the age of eighteen and joined the army. I had to return to England by troopship to do this. This voyage was more comfortable than the voyage out. I underwent six months' training at Aldershot. The army was a terrible let-down after the boys' service. I was a sergeant at Lovedale, but now I was a very lowly signalman, cleaning the latrines and peeling potatoes and doing any other menial task which they could find. At Lovedale we had been treated as gentlemen, but here I was treated as less than the dust. It was a terrible come down! The only bright spot about that six months was that Aldershot town was quite pleasant and I indulged in the off-duty extra curricular activities of the British Army wherever it is stationed —chasing the girls and drinking beer.

Eventually, much to my relief, training was over and without even a request from me I was posted back to India, where I was to stay for a nine-year stint.

After a brief stay in a camp in Bombay, my regiment was posted to the North West Frontier. I was thrilled at the prospect. Virtually, the only place at that time where there was any active service for a soldier in the Empire was on the North West Frontier. The Frontier had a romance about it, it was a real out-post of the Empire. The Pathans, formidable inhabitants of the area, were worthy foes, cunning, brave and dedicated to the destruction of their enemies, whether the enemies were fellow-tribesmen or the British. They are a remarkably handsome race, skilled in war, with peculiar ideas of honour and a lust to kill. They are also very patient, and a sniper would sit up in the rocks for days just waiting for an opportunity for an effective shot.

The Pathan is a strange mixture. He loves music and flowers and is desperately fond of children. He also treats animals very well and is a superb horseman. He

North West Frontier, Chitral region

does not talk very much, but has a pronounced, well developed, sense of humour. He makes a powerful and vicious enemy, but if a wrong can be settled without loss of honour then he is forgiving and courteous to his former foes. The Pathans have aristocratic looks and a swaggering confidence which is a pleasant change from the cringing subservience one encounters so much on the plains.

They were also notoriously cruel to their prisoners and devised all kinds of tortures. It was not advisable to be taken prisoner. I have often been struck by the similarity between the Pathans and the Apache Indians. They share the same pride, the same love of war and the same cruelty. Yes, they were worthy opponents and, as you can imagine, tales of their courage and their excesses were prolific and naturally became exaggerated in the telling.

The region round the Khyber Pass was absolutely suited to the tribesmen. It is a barren, inhospitable boulder-strewn area, full of gorges ideally suited to ambushes and guerilla warfare. It was just right for the Pathans who merged into the scenery and lived in caves and hollows in the mountains. I have seen a hillside one moment swarming with tribesmen and the next absolutely deserted, and it would happen so quickly that you would wonder if in fact you had been dreaming. It was a strange eerie campaign. I always had the feeling, particularly when patrolling near the Khyber, that we were being watched by hundreds of hostile eyes. It tended to be a war of nerves. The

enemy kept up the fighting at long distance. The Pathans took their women with them on their campaigns but they kept them completely concealed. I don't remember ever catching a glimpse of one Pathan woman during my nine years of patrolling in the area.

I remember, too, the freezing cold in the Khyber area. The cold in the Himalayas has a penetrating quality all its own. I remember the great struggle I had at night to keep warm. We used to dig holes in the ground and cover the holes with tarpaulin and heavy overcoats, and we used to sleep with heavy mufflers and head warmers on, but despite all this the cold penetrated to our very bones.

I soon learned that there was little romance in campaigning in the frontier areas. The miserable cold and the unpredictable enemy shattered all illusions about a romantic place to campaign.

In those days, in the early 1930's, I did not think too much about colonialism and the great agitation which was building up in India. I was a soldier, trained from the age of twelve to obey orders unquestioningly. I believed our function as the military in India was at all times to maintain law and order. To be perfectly honest, I was not too sure what the fighting was all about. The Pathans loved war-games and I knew that a holy man, the Fakir of Ipi, had stirred them up to rise against the British. The Pathans were in fact very anti-British and were determined to cause trouble on the frontier, and therefore they had to be contained and policed. The only time I felt any strong feelings against them was when reports came in of subhuman torture inflicted on soldiers unlucky enough to be captured. Boiling prisoners in water was one of their favourite tortures.

At this time there must have been about ten or twelve British regiments serving in India and as the political unrest developed the army was strengthened. It is, of course, a vast country and Indian regiments were also required to assist. The Indian regiments were made up of Hindus and Muslims with separate cook-houses and living quarters. The Indian regiments were officered by Indian British Viceroy's Commissioned Officers, not King's Commissioned Officers. We worked closely with the Indian regiments, but we lived separately.

Considering the primitive conditions on the frontier, with no amenities at all, it is interesting that the morale of the troops was so high. In the evenings after perhaps patrolling all day, we had nothing to do but sit in our dug-outs and play cards, smoke and plan what we would do on our return to the fleshpots.

I experienced action for the first time in this inhospitable terrain and was pleased that I wasn't too much of a coward. I was very frightened on each occasion that contact was made, but I found as so many others have found that I was more frightened of being afraid in front of my comrades than I was of the enemy. I still remember, however, the awful helplessness of crouching behind rocks while, from above, the tribesmen fired at us and the bullets pinged off the boulders all round us. We lost a number

of men largely due to ricochets. In fact more casualties were sustained from ricochets than from direct hits by bullets. A common danger often brings men closer together and close friendships can result. I, somehow, never had the capacity for this kind of friendship. In these long dark nights cooped up in holes in the ground with my fellow soldiers and with danger lurking not far away, the relation-ships formed were superficial. Our conversation was earthy and basic. The regular army in those days did not tend to attract into the ranks many with imagina-tion or great intelligence. At this superficial level I was at home with the roughest and toughest of men. I was big, strong and could stand up for myself. I think, however, the more sensitive part of my nature never came to terms with the coarseness and the ugliness of some aspects of army life. I don't wish to sound toffee-nosed about this, but there unquestionably was a part of me that never felt at ease in the rough, coarse *camaraderie* of the barracks.

I must have done quite well because I was promoted to lance corporal and was given charge of two pack-mules, two charging-batteries, a charging engine, a pair of binoculars, food for two mules and two privates, and sent up a mountain to establish a recording spot for sending back information about any visible move-ment of tribesmen.

The mules were the greatest problem. At times they got restless and we were petrified they would give away our position. Three of us would have proved easy prey for even a handful of Pathans.

One night one of the batteries, which was strapped to one of the mules, slipped, and the mule charged around in circles making the weirdest sounds of displeasure. We had visions of every Pathan in the area descending on us and we could almost feel the boiling water! However, we were lucky and we learned our lesson that before turning in for the night ourselves it was necessary to ensure that first of all the mules were comfortably settled.

I had nine years in this area. I suppose there was a rugged grandeur about the scenery. I do remember some spectacular sunsets and sunrises when the mountains were tinged with pink, and the huge boulders were a soft mauve or blue colour. However, nine years of this type of scenery, behind which danger lurked, soon lost its charm and we used to long for even the heat and dust of the plains.

We had bases just south of the foothills from which we operated from time to time. We patrolled in groups of nine or ten and as a result the battalion was strung over a wide area. Strangely enough, the bases were sited in RAF camps. The RAF used light aircraft which were used for flying over the mountains and observing the tribesmen. Our patrols were often geared to the results of these observation flights. Our patrol would last five or six days and then we would return to the camp. These were often quite pleasant interludes.

One very dramatic event which gave us a change of duty and which brought us, as soldiers, into a changed relationship with the frontiermen was the Quetta earthquake disaster. This occurred in 1934. We were stationed at Kohat at the time which was a long way from Quetta, but we could feel the fierce tremors and in fact heard rumblings in the far distance. Quetta was at the heart of the 'quake.

We were immediately moved by truck down to Quetta to help rescue people, and it was quite frightening as the earth was still shuddering and there was the constant fear of further tremors. We all had a feeling of great helplessness. As we neared Quetta we had to get down from the trucks as the roads were buckled and there were great gaping holes where the road should have been.

The place was absolutely devastated. It was as if a giant bulldozer had started at one end of the city and just destroyed all the buildings in its path. The place was a shambles and there was an ominous silence, broken only by the wailing of the bereaved as they found their dead relatives. For a long time afterwards I was haunted by the screams and unrestrained grief of the tribesmen as they uncovered their dead from the rubble-strewn streets.

The death-toll was enormous and until recent earthquakes the Quetta disaster was always quoted as one of the largest natural disasters of all time. I doubt if any exact figures of the casualties were ever produced, because I doubt if anyone recorded the number of dead. It was a ghost-city, and as night fell there was an eerie feeling, knowing that all around were probably corpses still undiscovered.

Our problem was where to start. There were no engineers to assist us and the water mains had burst. There were countless bodies buried in the débris, there was no food, and no medical supplies. Adding to the dilemma was the fact that we were in a hostile city where we could not expect any great gratitude for anything we did.

We spent a busy six to seven weeks in Quetta doing a variety of jobs, the main one being digging out bodies from amongst the fallen débris. We were frightened that cholera would break out, but we were fortunate and this did not happen. We repaired the water mains and we set up a tent-hospital. The RAF brought food, medical supplies and the other equipment we needed from Rawalpindi. Some of the tribesmen, after the initial surprise of seeing us in a new role, sold us eggs and chickens (at exorbitant prices!), and between the survivors of Quetta and ourselves there was an uneasy truce for the time we were there. There was nothing approaching friendship from a single one of them, but I think they were a trifle puzzled that this enemy could in fact be capable of caring for their sick and injured.

I think the Quetta experience had quite an effect on me. I saw human need for the first time at close quarters. I saw something of the fragility of human life. Some of the sights we saw in the ruins of Quetta were appalling. I spent a great deal of time with the injured and the dying. I did not see them as enemies or potential enemies, but as suffering humans and the better side of my nature was touched, and I was moved to do as much as I could for them. Army life can make one callous and hard, but I do not think it did that to me.

Chitral relief and Pathan warrior

The badly injured women and children affected me deeply. It was interesting for us to see another side to the tribesmen. Prior to this they had simply been implacable, hard foes, but we now saw them stricken with grief, and very helpless in the face of a disaster of such vast proportion. I think national disasters of the scale of Quetta inevitably raised the great question, 'Why does God allow so many to suffer, particularly children?' I have never found anyone who can give me a satisfactory answer to this question.

3 Romantic Interlude

Our battalion eventually left the Frontier and we were posted back to Jabbalpur, a place I knew so well. My parents were in Britain at this time, so it wasn't a home-coming for me.

Jabbalpur had one great attraction for all soldiers, the Anglo-Indian Railways Institute. It was a sizeable railway junction and provided one of the reasons, presumably, for installing the military centre there. In those days the railways were run by Anglo-Indians, and a right efficient job they did, too. Jobs were reserved for them in the railways, the posts and telegraph department and the army.

The British, I suppose, reserved these posts as a kind of sop to their consciences. There is no doubt that through the years they 'used' this community. The Anglo-Indian community did not just come into being by accident. The Portuguese were the first to realise the value of having a mixed-blood community at their disposal in their trading posts. The British followed the Portuguese example of encouraging their soldiers and clerks to marry Indian women and produce children whose loyalty to the East India Company would not be questioned. Financial inducements were even at one time offered.

This large colony of Anglo-Indians had the Institute as their club, and we had access to it. To use the modern terminology the Institute used to 'swing' on a Saturday night!

I have always had very close ties with Anglo-Indians and I would like to think I have a close understanding of the dilemma of this rather sad group of people who have in them the blood of two very diverse civilisations. Their dilemma is simply that of identity. What do they identify with, the British or European side of their ancestry or with the Indian side? Prior to 1947, before India gained her independence, all Anglo-Indians stressed their European heritage and lived their lives in a strange kind of vacuum. They were living in India, but were not of it. Their attitudes, of course, did not endear them to Indians generally. Especially the fact that they appeared to be a favoured race with jobs reserved for them in various Government posts.

At the time of civil unrest Anglo-Indians were involved with the police and the army in controlling mobs and in anti-riot squads. Their active participation in assisting the British-controlled pro-independence demonstrations did nothing to endear the community to the Indians. The idea of independence was anathema to all Anglo-Indians. Their identity with Britain went back to the creation of the community in the early seventeenth century. Independence to the Anglo-Indian meant fear of the unknown if not downright desertion by the British. Some of their leaders were to be very angry with the British for not negotiating safeguards for the community with the incoming Indian politicians. As it transpired, the community's leaders had to negotiate their own terms and were successful in having safeguards written into the new Constitution, safeguards which protected their language, religion and schools. They were the only minority community to be actually mentioned by name in the Constitution. With the benefit of hind-sight, we might say that the Anglo-Indian leaders probably did better on their own than if they had relied on a settlement arranged for them by the British.

The greatest problem facing Anglo-Indians, however, was that despite their loyal service in India to Britain in a number of spheres, they were never socially accepted by the British. Victorian standards died hard in India and, unlike the Dutch in the East Indies, the mixed race was kept in its place by very strict social barriers. The only exceptions to this were in the wealthiest families. Status and money did seem to make a difference, and very rich Anglo-Indians would be accepted in a limited way.

The social barriers increased when more and more wives came from Britain to stay with their husbands. These women, naturally, were more intolerant of the co-habitation of company officials and Indian women, and they even frowned on mixed marriages. The result was that the liaisons generally were continued secretly. The tea garden situation is a good example of this kind of problem. Young British tea planters, often in lonely isolated tea gardens were not allowed by their company rules to bring a wife out from Britain until they achieved the status of Senior Manager. This could take from twelve to fifteen years to achieve, so they made other arrangements, and the result was scores of Anglo-Indian children being born into a strange world where they weren't really accepted in either their fathers' or their mothers' society. This situation brought into being the Dr Graham's Homes, Kalimpong, and St George's Home, Ketti in South India, to help rescue these children from the neglect of the tea gardens.

The railway colonies were fascinating. This was an aspect of Anglo-Indian life at its most intriguing. The Anglo-Indian sitting rooms were full of faded photographs of grandpapa, an unsmiling mutton-chopped, moustachioed soldier, administrator, railway official, merchant, tea planter or whatever, who had dared to love out of his race and often out of his class. The men wore topis to work like the British and the women talked of Surbiton and Ealing, and they played cards and—above all—they had an infinite capacity to enjoy themselves. The Institute, therefore, on a Saturday night was the place to be. There was plenty of beer, and the Anglo-Indian girls are about the prettiest girls you will find anywhere in the world. One should not generalise I know, but in my experience the Anglo-Indian girls have far more character and grit than the men. They take the initiative and they often are the breadwinners.

It was in the Railway Institute in Jabbalpur that Cupid for the first time transfixed my large heart. One of the exciting features of going to the Institute on Saturday night was also the fact that fights broke out regularly between the soldiers and the Anglo-Indian lads who, not unnaturally, objected to their girls being ogled at or worse by the soldiers. Often bottles were used and I saw as much action in the Institute as I saw on the Frontier!

I had never been too interested in girls. I was a bit *gauche* and awkward in female company, largely because I had never had much opportunity to mix with the gentler sex.

Cecilia, however, knocked me for six. She was pretty with dark flashing eyes and the flawless skin which was part of the Indian in her and she evidently saw

something in me which she liked. She was a beautiful dancer as most Anglo-Indian girls are. She was full of rhythm and grace and, inexperienced as I was, I did not stand a chance. Her parents did not approve of their daughter getting mixed up with a common soldier; if I had been a sergeant it might have been different! Her mother had ambitions for her daughter and wished to use Cecilia's beauty to trap a more influential fish than Dudley Gardiner. We had, because of her parents' attitude, to meet secretly behind railway sheds, but I did not mind. I was head over heels in love and Cecilia could have trampled all over me if she wanted and I would not have objected. We decided to solve our problem by eloping! This meant that I would have to desert from the army, but I was prepared to do that for my Cecilia. Considering how respectful to discipline I had been all these years, it shows what the power of love can do. We decided we would run as far away from Jabbalpur as we could, and decided that Assam would be a good haven for us. Cecilia had relatives living in Jorhat whom she felt would be sympathetic and harbour us.

On the fateful day, I walked out of the barracks, went down to the Institute where Cecilia was waiting with her bits and pieces, and we went to the station and took the first of a series of trains, which finally deposited us in Assam. I was so besotted with love that to begin with the enormity of my crime as regards the army, never mind as regards Cecilia and her parents, never crossed my mind.

As Cecilia had predicted, her relatives

(who were poor folk living in a house which could be better described as a hut) accepted us. They were quite tickled at having a European to stay with them, despite the fact that he was a rather pathetic specimen without any money.

I worked in the rice fields and after the rigidly structured life of the army, the almost idyllic pastoral life was a pleasant interlude. I enjoyed going back to Cecilia at night and I felt healthy and fulfilled. There was at the back of my mind, however, a niggling doubt—what happens next? We obviously would not stay where we were for ever and a day but to return to India could be risky as the army are always very loth to give up their own!

Anyway the problem was dramatically solved for me. One evening Cecilia was in bed looking her most attractive and I was sitting on the edge of the bed removing my boots, when a military policeman abruptly entered the room and asked me, 'What are you doing'. This was really a stupid question, but it elicited from me an even more stupid answer, 'I'm learning Urdu!' I replied. I just said the first thing that came into my head!

This was the end of my romantic interlude. Cecilia got the fright of her life, and eventually returned, duly penitent, to her parents, while I found myself escorted by two MP's back to Jabbalpur, to be tried for desertion. At this stage I realised the stupidity of my action and frankly Cecilia did not seem to be worth all the trouble I had got myself into. On the train I was well and truly guarded, even when I went to the toilet. The MP's thought I might jump the train.

I was court-martialled for desertion. The defending officer, who need not be a lawyer but usually knows you and can say something helpful in your defence, was very young and inexperienced. He did not do a very good job of defending me. My defence was very simple and was that I had served nine years in the Frontier and during that time had been deprived of all feminine company and, in seeing this girl, I was bewitched to such an extent my better judgement was affected and being a bit fed up with the army decided to elope with her. I did add that I was very sorry for what I had done.

The Judge, who was a bemedalled Lt Colonel, had been a long time in Jabbalpur. It was a long time too since he had heard a shot fired in anger. He had a reputation for toughness and my heart sank as the trial proceeded and my defence lawyer really did nothing to help me. I had been in desertion for three months, four days and six hours. And so the Colonel's sentence was that I should go to Lahore Central Jail for that same time. I spent the three months picking ochre for mattresses and I detested every moment of it; I found the restriction on my freedom of movement the hardest part to take. The jail was quite clean, but the prison authorities made us work very hard. I think they went on the principle that the more tired we prisoners were the less trouble we could be. I heartily disliked prison and determined I would never blot my copybook again.

I suppose in deserting I had shown a bit of rebellious spirit, but from my time in jail, I was determined to conform to the army discipline and to play the game according to the rules laid down by the army. I have never regretted doing this and I was finally to sever my connection with the army after 36 years of service.

4 The Death Railway

Shortly after I came out of jail, war was declared with Nazi Germany and immediately all British troops who could be spared were withdrawn from the Empire to return to Britain to help in the European theatre of war. I flew back to Britain in a seaplane. Flying was pretty crude in these days and it took twelve days to fly from Bombay to England. Flying was still a hazardous way of travelling in these days and flying boats were cumbersome and slow. I was really very glad when the flight was over, although it had been in its own way an exhilarating experience.

Once more I was back in Hounslow Barracks. The barracks, however, had been renovated and some of the older buildings knocked down and replaced.

I was then posted to Parkhurst Barracks on the Isle of Wight near the famous Parkhurst Prison. Here I started to train National Servicemen, having been exalted to the rank of corporal. I was in charge of squads of forty men and responsible for training them as quickly as possible into something resembling soldiers. Time was not on our side. It was quite a pleasant posting however. The recruits were eager to pass out, and my two stripes commanded respect along with the fact that I had served in the North West Frontier, of which I reminded them from time to time. There was a very happy social life in Parkhurst town which we all enjoyed. This pleasant little interlude was short-lived, however, as after a brief spell in Aldershot I was posted back to the Far East.

Meanwhile my father had done well in the army and was now a Captain and had hopes of promotion to Major. My mother by this time was a hopeless cripple and as a consequence life at home was not very happy. They lived, of course, in better quarters but my mother was a querulous invalid and my father, never the most patient man, was not very patient with her.

Cemetery at El Alamein, where DG's father is buried

The day I left for Aldershot and embarkation I left early and went to say good-bye to them. I gave my mother a hearty kiss and my father a peck on the nose. Little did I realise that this would be the last time I would see either of them.

My father was eventually posted to the Middle East and my mother was sent by my father to an encampment near Bognor Regis. One night when Southampton was being bombed a single German bomber jettisoned its bombs when chased by British night-fighters and the coach where my mother was staying was just blown away. She had led a sad life, and I remember her with affection. She was in her later years rarely without pain and so I tried to think of her death as a merciful release from much suffering. I prefer to remember her not as the complaining invalid but as the young girl who laughed a lot, who was the popular barmaid at the Roebuck Hotel.

My father did not survive her for long. He was present at El Alamein and was killed a short distance from the battlefield by a mortar shell and is buried in El Alamein cemetery, which I have visited. I was captured by the Japanese just before he was killed and I was mistakenly reported killed in action, and I am haunted by the thought that perhaps he died thinking that I too had perished as had his wife. I wondered if the thought that the two of us had died perhaps made him reckless and led to his own end. It is probably stupid to speculate, but it is difficult sometimes to control one's thoughts. My father was an efficient soldier. His promotion from the ranks proves this. He was not an easy man to know. I cannot claim there was any great bond of affection between us, but I respected him. I see much of myself in him and the fact that I found out about his death when I came out of the prison camp three years later did nothing to soften the blow.

But, to return to my story, we had embarked on the *Oronsay* at Liverpool and to avoid U-Boats, twisted and turned on our way down the African coast, finally landing in Durban. We caused havoc there. We had been cooped up in the troopship for weeks and in over-crowded conditions and Durban with its lights, food, bars and night clubs was like paradise. We were in endless trouble with the local police because we cared nothing for the rules of *apartheid*, and it was the African bars and brothels which attracted us. This led to all kinds of confrontations. From Durban we sailed to Bombay and then to Bahrain in the Persian Gulf. From there we embarked on another ship for Bombay and yet again I landed back in Jabbalpur. I felt very much at home there. The war in the Pacific, however, was going very badly. The Japanese were literally pouring through the Pacific Islands and Australia was threatened, as was Singapore.

We were drafted to Madras and sailed for Singapore to reinforce the garrison. We knew we were sailing into trouble but like everyone else we believed the stories about how impregnable Singapore was, and our morale as a consequence was high despite the fact that the 'Japs' by this time were pouring in from Thailand and swarming all over the peninsula.

We were stationed at Fort Canning and stayed only ten days as the 'Japs' made for the causeway which attaches Singapore Island to the mainland of Malaysia. Despite the disorganisation amounting to panic in some quarters, we still felt that the island could be defended, but the general morale of units around us was appalling and no one seemed to be giving orders. The causeway was blown up but the 'Japs' came across in boats and as soon as largish numbers of them gained a footing on the island, the writing was very much on the wall. Some units, including ours, fought as best they could but others seemed just unable to cope with the unorthodox tactics of the little yellow men.

We were lucky in that our officers still remained in control of us despite the collapsing situation and we were evacuated by sea to Rangoon. We thus prolonged our freedom for a little. Singapore was a disgrace, and the British could take little credit from the events there. Australians I was to meet later in the prison camp were very bitter at the whole handling of the situation.

As soon as we reached Rangoon we were moved into a camp at Pegu about 140 miles from Rangoon. Burma is a very lush and beautiful country. I had always wanted to visit Burma, unfortunately this was hardly the time to take in the beauty of the country. I had always imagined the Burmese to be very gracious easy-going people and nothing that happened later caused me to change this opinion.

By this time I had been promoted to Warrant Officer. The Indian Army 62nd and 63rd Brigades were with us at Pegu, and we prepared to meet the full might of the very mobile Japanese Army which had been unleashed in Burma. The jungles around Pegu were alive with them. There appeared to be thousands and thousands of them. We resisted for a time but they moved so quickly as they were not burdened with heavy kit and seemed to be able to go for days without much rest or food. They excelled in jungle warfare. They seemed to merge into the dense foliage. Their courage too was undisputed. They did not fear death, only disgrace.

Our casualties were mounting rapidly and those who were in forward positions were summoned back to Company Head-quarters and we prepared to defend a very limited perimeter defence. We discovered at this time that the rest of our forces had gone beyond Pegu and had broken out to the Chindwin River and had made it into the Chin Hills thence into India. We were the unlucky ones. It became obvious on 13 April 1942, that the situation was desperate. I was with a detachment of Gurkhas and we were told to destroy our equipment and just wait for the enemy to appear. The Gurkha is a fierce warrior and for him just to sit and wait for capture was incomprehensible. I was not too pleased about the order either, but our casualties had been very high. I had only twenty-five men left in my detachment. I was concerned for the Gurkhas' safety—the Japanese really hated them—and so I took my little party to Tongoo in the hope that

Bringing in wounded, near Rangoon

we might find a way through the 'Jap' lines. We had no luck, however, as we ran smack into a large patrol at Tongoo and we surrendered to them. I had a rather bad infection in my leg and they treated me quite reasonably to begin with. The Gurkhas, as I feared, were badly treated but they showed as always great courage despite the manhandling they received.

There was a railway line near the house where they dressed my leg, and hundreds of British prisoners were herded on to the line as they were rounded up from the nearby jungle. Eventually a train appeared and we were taken on open railway 'flats' very slowly across the Salween River and we were deposited in Moulmein Jail. It was in a filthy condition. We were all dead-tired, filthy, naturally depressed beyond measure, and frightened as to what fate would befall us. The Japanese made no secret of their delight in having so many European prisoners. They firmly believed their own propaganda that they were winning splendid victories over the decadent and soft Europeans and they were determined to enjoy their feeling of superiority.

At this time the 'Japs' wished to build a railway from Bangkok to Moulmein to facilitate the movement of troops and food. Their lines of communication were stretched to the limit and so the Burma-Siam Railway, which was to cause so many deaths, was planned and the Japs decided to use prisoner-labour. It has been called, most aptly, the death railway. It claimed thousands of lives. It was quite an engineering feat to carve this new railway through the dense jungle. The

Soldiers of a Gurkha regiment

'Japs' wanted the railway to be operational as quickly as possible, so there was tremendous pressure on their own troops to push the construction gangs to the limit.

The numbers in Moulmein grew and grew. A large number of Australians who had escaped from Malaysia into Burma were brought to the jail. Soon there were about four to five thousand men in the jail. There were no officers as the officers had been segregated from us. We were a right mixture, Indians, Australians, Gurkhas, British, Burmese and a few Ceylonese. The overcrowding was dreadful and sickness started right from the beginning. The 'Japs' had little in the way of medical supplies and their food supplies, too, were limited. We lived on watery boiled rice and lentils. There was a feeling of hopelessness amongst the prisoners generally. The weather was steaming hot and the Monsoon was just about to break. Tempers were short and right from the beginning the Australians with minds of their own, made it clear that they wanted to rule the roost. Rules, as far as they were concerned, were meant to be broken.

I worked in a working party in a leper colony for a few days. This colony was situated near Moulmein Jail. We were sent down to build latrines for the lepers. They had some Indian and Burmese doctors looking after them.

It struck me at the time that although the work was hard, it was a kind of Christian act to help these poor deformed afflicted people. My faith somehow strengthened in the prison camps.

Just three of the many who suffered at the hands of the Japanese

Every morning at dawn we were paraded, and the 'Japs' made us bow three times to the rising sun. During that time when there was quietness I used to say my prayers and this helped me to go through this ritual without feeling I was betraying my beliefs.

I remember working in the colony one Sunday morning, digging away as usual, when along came a car with a big balloon gas bag on the roof. The 'Japs' were very short of petrol and used gas to run their cars. A very small Japanese officer got out of the car. I remember his sword seemed to be extra long. To our surprise he came over to the trench and looking down said 'You Christian?' I answered rather hesitantly, 'Yes'. He said 'You should be in church, come'. So we clambered out of the trench and followed him into a ruined church which had been almost completely destroyed by allied bombing. We said prayers and sang some well-known hymns. The Japanese officer bent his head in prayer all the time, and then suddenly left the church, got into his car and drove away. It was a strangely heartening incident during a very bleak period.

Eventually, and with some relief on my part, most of us were moved out of Moulmein Jail to work on the railway. Moulmein Jail was depressing in the extreme and, bad though the railway was to be, I certainly felt better out in the jungle camps. I enjoyed my second spell in prison even less than my first. The camp was called Camp Forty (Niki) and was in the Valley of the Three Pagodas and this camp, which we first of all had to construct out of bamboo and other

materials supplied by the Japanese, was to be my home for three and a half long years. At least I survived.

The first thing the Japanese did was to separate the Europeans from the Indians and Burmese. This seemed a strange thing to do. It was almost a recognition on their part of a difference between us. There did not appear to be much difference in the treatment meted out to both groups though the Indians suffered even worse from disease than we did and, as I have said, there was an acute shortage of medicine.

The Japanese discovered that I was the senior rank amongst the three thousand men in the camp, including the Australians, and they nominated me Liaison Officer between the Japanese and the European prisoners. In other words, the 'Japs' informed me what work had to be done and I informed the men through a Committee which we formed, which was made up of NCO's, what work had to be done for the day. There was no language barrier because the 'Japs' had American educated interpreters who spoke English with broad Brooklyn accents. The job of Liaison Officer was a very tiresome one and got me into all kinds of trouble not only with the Japanese but with the prisoners as well.

The Japanese Commander made it clear to me right from the beginning that he would hold me personally responsible for any obstructive difficulties the prisoners might cause on our section of the railway. The Commander had his instructions from above and the allocation of the railway line he had to build in a prescribed time. In fact the whole line was scheduled by the Engineers to be completed in a year.

The Australians never appreciated the awkward position I was in and were constantly causing trouble. The Japanese guards were really quite thin on the ground. The terrain was almost sufficient to be our prison itself. To escape in that area would have meant certain death from natural causes, if a Japanese patrol did not carry out a summary execution. Because of the lack of supervision, the Australians particularly annoyed the 'Japs' by taking no care with their work, and laid the plates and lines carelessly and caused accidents. They thought they were being brave heroes, defying the Japanese, but I suffered tremendously from this attitude.

Three times in three months I was sentenced to death. I will never forget the first night I was informed I would be shot first thing in the morning because of an incident involving Australians. I spent a grim night. I could not sleep. It seemed to me such a stupid waste to die because of the mock-heroics of others. Life seemed very precious, and I was tempted to beg for mercy of my captives and, but for the fact that others would have witnessed this weakness, I would have probably done so.

At dawn they came for me. Three grim-faced 'Japs' who prodded me with the butt of their rifles. They took me to the perimeter of the camp and halted me before a newly-dug grave. I was sweating with fear and I was convinced this was my last moment on earth. I hastily said a prayer asking God for forgiveness for my many weaknesses. I expected some immediate action but we waited, the 'Japs' still grim-faced, and me shivering with fearful anticipation. A Japanese officer arrived and on his order the soldiers withdrew some paces and levelled their rifles at me and I prepared to die. The officer gave the order to fire, and there was only a click followed by loud raucous laughter from the 'Japs'. Their rifles were empty. I was marched back to the hut and told that this should be a lesson to me. Three times in all, this pantomime was repeated in the ensuing months. It was no less difficult to take the other times than it was the first. The only explanation I can give as to why I was spared is that the Japanese Commander and I got on reasonably well. I think he realised that I was doing my best to help my men survive in the jungle by being reasonably co-operative with our captors.

The Japanese, particularly the Koreans amongst them, were cruel in the extreme. We also had some Thai guards who were very fair and even gentle. Thailand was an unwilling ally of the Japanese. To save their country being ravaged by the Japanese the Thai Government collaborated with them.

The 'Japs' reserved the worst torture for the Gurkhas, perhaps the only allied soldiers who were their match man to man in the jungle. I have seen Gurkhas with their heads tied in gunny bags being chased round trees and used for bayonet practice. I have also seen Gurkhas stripped naked, which for a caste Hindu was a terrible disgrace in itself, and planted up to their necks in the ground

Prisoner-of-war camp at Tamuang in Thailand

and then their heads were smeared with resin or grease and they were left to the mercy of the ants. To protect my men from these incidents I was prepared to be co-operative with the 'Japs' as far as work-programmes were concerned. I used to remonstrate just as fiercely with the 'Japs' as I did with the Australians. As I have said, I think the Japanese Commander realised that I wanted the best for my men and the minimum amount of trouble.

The 'Japs' themselves were very short of supplies of all kinds. Although our food was appallingly inadequate, so to a certain extent was theirs. We lost great numbers because of sickness and so did they.

The diet consisted of noodles, cabbage soup, chapattis and sometimes boiled rice. A great number of the prisoners lost their teeth because of the lack of calcium in the diet.

To let you know how low we could sink to obtain food, I remember American B29 bombers had sunk a considerable amount of Japanese shipping in the Gulf of Siam. We were taken to the beaches to collect the bodies of the dead seamen which were being washed up on the beach. The Japanese greatly respect their dead and built small shrines for each of the corpses. We discovered that the corpses attracted offal and underneath the armpits and in the crotches, prawns and shrimps gathered, so we waded out with tins tied round our necks and gathered the shrimps and prawns and enjoyed a tasty change to our diet, and tried to forget where they came from! We often used to secretly raid the Japanese officers' dustbins looking for their left-overs which we were not too proud to eat.

For three and a half years we worked seven days a week pushing this railway through the most inhospitable terrain, foot by foot. The Monsoon period was the worst time. The Monsoon in Burma is particularly heavy and depressing. Day after day it poured with rain. We suffered from all kinds of skin disease, from dysentery, beri-beri and fever of all descriptions. We lost weight and some of the men were like walking skeletons. The regular soldiers had a slight edge on the National Servicemen when it came to survival. For one thing we had been toughened I suppose by years in the army. We had never had a soft life and my years in the North West Frontier were excellent preparation for the hardships of the jungle. Above all, I think as regulars we were more mentally prepared for the pressures and isolation of a prison camp. We were used to being away from families for long periods. We were used to amusing ourselves in an inhospitable setting and I think as a result we adapted better to the appalling conditions.

My health was quite reasonable. I had dysentery at times, as everyone had, but I kept myself as clean as possible, and there certainly was plenty of exercise available and, although the food was unappetising, I was used to Indian food and found it reasonably nourishing.

The Japanese, sometimes in fits of temper, would ill-treat us. A Japanese guard was mysteriously killed and no amount of beatings and interrogation solved the mystery of who the killer was.

British prisoners of war

The 'Japs' retaliated by giving us no food for some days and very much reduced rations for a further period. The guards often carried iron bars and the prisoners were struck by them frequently. Prisoners were put in bamboo cages and starved and tormented by food being placed just outside their reach. Most of the time, however, I think the Japanese were just as fed up as we were. They had been posted to the back-of-beyond and away from the bright lights of cities like Rangoon and Singapore. They were also far away from home, and Japanese family life is very close-knit.

There must have been about three thousand deaths on the railway and I know a great number of those who survived have been dogged by ill-health ever since their ordeal. Most of those who died were buried beside the railway, including the Japanese. After the war the War Graves Commission recovered a number of the bodies and buried them in a very beautiful cemetery in Thanbyusiat which curiously the Japanese created themselves. The Australians, British and Indians are buried there. Many thousands of civilians also perished as they too were used to push the railway through. I think this is a fact which is sometimes overlooked.

Right in the centre of the Thanbyusiat Cemetery, is a large cross, made by prisoners from tree trunks. There is an archway entrance to the cemetery on which is written in English, Hindi and Japanese:
'When you go home, tell them of us and say, for their tomorrow, we gave our today'.

As you enter the cemetery you see the rows and rows of graves going up the hill, a very large hill, all white stones seemingly stretching for miles.

Those of us who survived those dreadful days have many memories, some horrible in the extreme, others of great tenderness. The conditions brought out all that is worst in men, and also all that is good. The bestiality of the Japanese is well known. But often our men, because of acute deprivations and the human instinct to survive stooped to crimes they would never have undertaken in normal circumstances. On the other hand I could relate countless stories of sheer heroism and self-sacrifice; for example, of men doing double work to assist sick comrades, and sometimes of men taking beatings in place of friends as they knew the next beating would prove fatal.

A very well-known headmaster in a Scottish school, when asked to define education, used his experience on the railway to define it. He related that he was a scholar with a degree in Classics from Oxford which was absolutely no use to him in the jungle. He would not have survived the ordeal if he had not been protected and helped by an illiterate Australian who, as a civilian, used to drive cattle in the North West Territory of Australia. He used to drive the cattle long distances and learned to live off the land as he drove the herd north to Darwin. He taught the headmaster to survive in the jungle; how to build a *basha* with leaves, what to eat from the jungle and what not to eat. In return for this, at night in the camp, the headmaster taught the

Australian to read and to write, and every Christmas he still receives a letter written in the careful copperplate he taught him in that most inhospitable jungle. I like that story because even in the most desperate conditions the human spirit can often not just survive but rather magnificently surmount the problems. Surely, the exchange of skills is what education is all about?

In a strange way I don't regret my experiences on the railway. I came out of that experience a wiser man with a far greater insight into human strengths and human weakness. I learned to appreciate the small things in life, things I had tended to take for granted before: a square meal, peace of mind, privacy, a comfortable bed, to name a few.

I was lonely in the camp. I had really no friends. My position as Liaison Officer of course isolated me from the others. To be responsible for three thousand men was a terrible responsibility. Certainly some of the senior NCO's helped me considerably, but the overall responsibility was still mine.

The great dilemma on which the Australians and I differed was on what our policy should be as regards the construction of the railway. They were determined to sabotage the railway at every conceivable opportunity, regardless of the cost to their fellow prisoners. My philosophy was different. I felt strongly that the railway would be completed anyway, and it was my duty to see as far as was humanly possible that as many men as possible survived the ordeal of the jungle. If this meant working to Japanese

orders concerning the railway, then I felt this was justified. This, in no way meant 'kow towing' at all times to our captors. I was never guilty of that. I was a professional soldier. They were also professional soldiers, and we had a reasonable working relationship, which was strained a great number of times, but did result in positive action by them at times to our seriously ill and wounded.

The railway was completed just about the time the war in Burma took a turn for the better. I remember too the terrible feeling of anticlimax when a guard said to me one day 'The war is almost over'. It seemed such a simple statement and, strangely enough, so conditioned was I by this type of life in the jungle, that I was almost disappointed that I was to leave the known environment—despite the deaths, the disease, the misery. Later I did feel some elation when we were moved back to Moulmein Jail. Clearly, it wasn't just a rumour. The guards were on edge, nervous, and anxious to treat us well. In Moulmein Jail there was chaos, the Japanese Army was falling back on all fronts, from Kohima in Assam and from the Chinese border. They were a demoralised army. Our guards suddenly left us. They obviously feared reprisals. We opened the gate of the jail and took boats across the river and walked as far as possible to a place called Thaton where we met up with Force 136, an advance guard of British soldiers air-dropped in advance of the main army.

I discovered two shattering facts. Firstly, I had been reported killed in action and I was to discover it was to take me quite a time to prove my identity, and secondly, I was given the shattering news that both my parents had been killed. This was a real blow. Weakened physically as I was by my three and a half years in the camp, I found this news hard to accept. I was drunk for the best part of two weeks before I eventually came to terms with the fact of their deaths. Their deaths meant that I had literally no-one left in the world. I was alone and really felt isolated and a little bit desperate.

What happened next did not help the situation in any way. I was sent down to a Field Security post on the Chindwin River. I discovered that some of my former comrades in the camp must have been giving adverse reports about me. A young man, a homosexual, who I think was an Anglo-Indian and had collaborated with the Japanese to the extent of living with them also had it in for me. He himself was being thoroughly questioned and probably to take some of the heat away from himself, he made up all kinds of stories about me. Fortunately, he was obviously such a mixed up, paranoid creature that the Security Officer did not pay much heed to his accusations against me.

I also discovered that the Security people used three colours to denote gradings. A person graded white was not under suspicion, grey meant under suspicion and black meant a confirmed quisling and co-operator with the enemy. There were a surprisingly large number in this latter category. I was questioned and re-questioned over a three- to four-week period and finally the authorities were

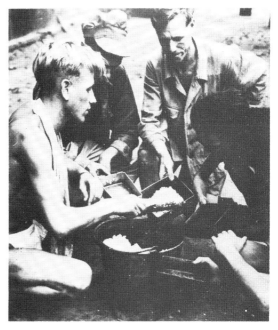

Last meal of rice for POWs in Rangoon prison

Lord Louis Mountbatten, Supreme Allied Commander, talking to Australian ex-POWs

Rangoon pagodas provide exotic background for strolling soldiers

satisfied with my story and much to my relief I was graded white.

I was sent to Rangoon where the ex-prisoners were waiting for ships to take them home, in most cases to joyful reunions with relatives and friends. I was asked if I wanted to go back to the United Kingdom but I had not recovered from the loss of my parents and, anyway, I had no relations or even close friends to go back to, so I elected to stay on in Rangoon. It was also hinted that the army would like me to stay because of my knowledge of signals installations. The Japanese had left a great deal of signal equipment behind and one of my jobs was to dismantle the equipment and salvage what was useful.

The United Kingdom really did not have any great pull for me. I suppose after so long in India I had become 'Asianised'. I was used to the East, felt at home in it, and liked to feel the warmth of the sun on my broad back. I felt at home with Asian people, I could talk to them in coffee shops and in the bazaars, and they seemed to relate easily to me despite my white skin.

There was a great deal of work to be done in Army Headquarters and I enjoyed my work there, and as a consolation I was promoted first of all to Lieutenant and then to Captain. I was glad of this promotion because it proved to me at least that my record was absolutely clean and that my actions in the camp had been vindicated.

The one exciting event of that spell in Rangoon was the assassination of Aung Sang, the hero of Burma. This caused a great political upheaval and once more

Aung Sang, hero of Burma

the army was back to its peace-time role of policing political demonstrations. I eventually moved to Mingladon and was involved in training the Karens who would take over from us when Burma would gain her independence in 1948. The Karens, however, were not popular in Burma as a whole and the country was full of dissatisfaction and unrest. They were eventually forced underground when General Ne Win took over and all our trainees disappeared overnight into the jungle and carried on an effective guerilla campaign against successive governments and régimes.

We were given forty-eight hours to leave the country and the authorities had the difficult task of deciding where to send us. We were put on ships and landing craft and sent to Singapore. We were not particularly welcome there as Singapore had its full complement of troops garrisoned on the island. Somehow or other we were assimilated into the Singapore garrison.

It was rather ironic that after all we had suffered in Burma, we had to leave the country so hurriedly and so ignominiously. It did not seem quite fitting. Burma, naturally, will always be remembered by me. To have been part of one of the most dramatic and most horrific incidents of World War II means something to me. David Lean's film 'Bridge Over the River Kwai' has, of course, stirred great interest in the railway.

I think I can honestly say that I have no hatred in my heart for the Japanese, and the superior attitude of the whites generally must have goaded the 'Japs' to excesses. Having said that, their cruelty must be deplored. As with all situations, however, one cannot generalise. There were some reasonably humane guards but I must admit they were in the minority. These days are far away and the holocaust of Hiroshima and Nagasaki surely set the account straight with a vengeance.

5 Post War Unrest

I seemed somehow to attract trouble; the Malayan anti-Communist campaign started soon after we arrived on the island of Singapore. Communist guerillas infiltrated from Thailand and started making a nuisance of themselves down the length of the peninsula. British lives were in danger as rubber planters and their wives on isolated plantations were amongst the targets selected by the Communists. Military historians are already claiming that this Malayan anti-guerilla campaign was a model campaign. If the Americans had paid more heed to the methods used, they might have been more successful in Vietnam.

Singapore, of course, was a soldier's dream for a night out. Amusement complexes like the New World catered for all tastes, dance halls, bars etc. We spent a lot of money, drank a lot, and enjoyed the local girls. Swimming was my favourite pastime and in the warm waters around the island I developed into a remarkable distance swimmer, swimming about five miles and ending up usually in Johore Village, at a pleasant little Chinese Bar. Those were good days, but once again the popularity of the army was waning. In wartime soldiering was a respectable occupation. Soldiers were needed and the general population was grateful. In peacetime, of course, it is different. The army is never respected in the same way. Mark you, I was an officer now and as an officer the social life in Singapore was quite hectic. I must say it was pleasant to be able to go into the famous Raffles Hotel as an officer and enjoy a drink and feel reasonably at home. Despite my commission, however, I was never comfortable in the cocktail scene. I was blunt and said what I thought, and I soon found that frankness is not considered by some a social asset. I therefore opted out of the high flying social set which many of the officers joined. I enjoyed my swimming, my beer, and I became an avid reader. I

Brass band at head of parade celebrating liberation of Singapore

spent a good deal of money building up a library of sorts. I was never lonely if I had a good book to hand. I do not think I was considered standoffish. I was probably regarded as a bit odd by some of my fellow officers. They probably put my attitude down to the fact that I had come up from the ranks, a fact of which I made no secret.

One friend I did make in Singapore lives quite close to me here in Calcutta, in the same street in fact. He was Warrant Officer Toogood, MBE, and he runs an escort service between Calcutta and Nepal. I had other friends but because I stayed out in the East, contact has been lost over the years.

The area was eventually posted to in Malaysia with signal equipment was a relatively quiet area and contact with the guerillas was minimal. I was quite glad of this. In my early days in the North West Frontier, being young and enthusiastic, I had longed for action to test myself. After years of service in the army, I was now no longer enthusiastic about seeking out the action.

I was very sad when in 1950 my stint in Singapore came to an end and I was posted to the Middle East, to a camp twenty miles outside Ismailia on the Suez Canal. Our duties were purely and simply the occupation of the British Canal Zone. We also trained young national service-men who were posted to us and patrolled around the canal area.

As always, I soon developed a routine. I inherited a bull terrier and he gave me a lot of pleasure and a lot of exercise. He was called Clefty which means in Arabic 'thief', and he was that all right. He used to wage a personal vendetta against all cats, and the desert cats could be very vicious. He had lots of scars, the result of many scraps on the outskirts of the camp. In the early evening I would take him the mile and a half to the canal, where he would swim and I would sit on the bank and watch the ships go past. I would then return to the canteen, have some beer, and then retire early to my very pleasant quarters and read.

I became interested in the Middle East and its complicated history. The desert has a strange beauty all its own. It is a harsh place, stark and uninviting at times, and yet at sunrise and sunset—with the constant interplay of light and shade amongst the dunes—the desert can be beautiful in the extreme. I could, however, never feel the same way about Egypt as I could about India. India enthralls me emotionally, the Middle East interests me as the cradle of civilisation. One cannot live in a country like Egypt without being stirred intellectually. There are constant reminders of the greatness of Egypt's past, and Egypt's contribution to man's development. I began to read a great deal about the area, and have subsequently written some articles about it.

I was moved to Fayid Camp which was an RAF Camp where the living conditions were far superior to the normal army quarters. I have very happy memories of the camp and some very pleasant Sunday jaunts in various aircraft to the Persian Gulf, where we would fish, picnic, have some beer and return to base before dark. Fayid was a big station, housing about four thousand RAF personnel and fifty of us. It was the main air base for a very large area. There was very little hint of the trouble which was soon to erupt round the canal and envelop most of the Arab countries and Israel.

Our main campaign was directed against thieves. The Egyptians were past-masters in the art of stealing. Apart from the normal thieving one finds in many army camps, the Egyptians were after copper and brass cables. On the black market these metals were priceless. The thieves used to grease their bodies and wear only a loin cloth so that if they were caught they still stood a chance of escape by slipping out of the grasp of their captors.

The rising popularity of **General** Nasser caused difficulties. Despite the problems he was to cause he undoubtedly gave the Egyptians some pride. He roused their national spirit and although this was largely concentrated against Israel, we British in the occupying force came in for our fair share of abuse. His decision to nationalise the canal meant our with-drawal. I was one of the last to move out of the canal and one of the interesting duties I had was to sell surplus Air Force stores to the local contractors. I learned all about hard-headed businessmen and the whole fascinating possibilities of bartering. I would at the time of the sale of a particular piece of equipment, say a truck, think I had done very well out of the deal for the RAF. I would then discover that the purchaser had sold the vehicle to someone else for double what he had given me. I was to find this

experience very valuable indeed when I had to buy bulk food supplies for my feeding programme in India. The merchants in India are well known for their business acumen and their sharp-dealing, but, in my experience, compared to the Egyptian contractors they are not in the same league.

After this task was completed I was posted from the Canal Zone to Cyprus. I have one sad memory of that move. Because of severe quarantine restrictions I was prevented from taking Clefty with me. I felt that I could just not leave him behind to perhaps be abused by the locals, so before I left the mess for the last time, I called Clefty and shot him with my revolver. I felt dreadful. I decided there and then that I would never own another dog. I still feel some guilt when I think of Clefty. You cannot really explain your actions to an animal. You cannot say, 'Look here, I'm going to shoot you. It's really for your own good.'

In Cyprus, life was very quiet and the island was very beautiful. I was in a camp at Episkopé which was perched on the cliffs, on the north side of the island, and I was in a tented site right on the cliff edge so that when I woke in the morning I looked out to the blue Mediterranean. Deep blue it was, Oxford blue, and it is small wonder to me that the gods made their home in Greece. The combination of blue sea and blue sky, and the muted tones of the olive trees and the white sun-splashed houses set into the coves and the hill sides still evoke in me the happiest of memories. The swimming, of course, was superb and after the monotonous flatness of the Canal Zone, the hills and the variety of scenery in Cyprus was enchanting.

The peace and quiet were short lived. Archbishop Makarios and General Grivas saw to that and the EOKA freedom movement was soon in full swing. I seemed to attract nationalistic movements wherever I went! Our job once again was to maintain law and order. The aims of EOKA were complicated by various factors, not the least of these being the fact that two communities were involved; Greek Cypriots and Turkish Cypriots. They were, however, united in wanting the British removed.

We had quite a hair-raising time running convoys back and forward to Famagusta where our supplies came from. Civil unrest and urban guerilla warfare are disliked intensely by the military. It was rather like being back on the Frontier living in the midst of a hostile civil population. The methods of EOKA were a bit more sophisticated than the Pathan sitting up in the rock round the Khyber waiting for a favourable target.

About this time French troops started to arrive in Cyprus. The Suez Canal had been nationalised and the British and French Governments made no secret that they wished to rectify this situation. We knew without being told that something was afoot which obviously involved the Canal Zone. We found the French troops very amiable to work and live with. The officers were particularly charming and we used to have some rip-roaring evenings in the mess. I have never seen so much wine drunk in my life. They even drank

wine with their breakfast. They used to drink a full bottle the way I would drink a bottle of water. I must say they stood up to this very well indeed and, if they were alcoholics, they gave no sign of incompetence or even being mildly affected by their excesses.

I was once more posted to the United Kingdom and the blow of leaving beautiful Cyprus was softened by the fact that I was promoted to Major. When I obtained this rank I felt I had achieved something. I had come from the ranks, and although I knew I would be unlikely to progress further I felt proud that I had made it beyond the rank of Captain. My next posting was to West Germany, to a place called Herfud, where we underwent extensive manoeuvres with the American Army to prepare for the proposed invasion of the Canal Zone.

In October 1956 we returned to Cyprus to the RAF base at Akrotirir not far from Nicosia, and we waited for instructions to move into the Middle East. Rumours of course were rife as to where exactly we were going. The rumours were resolved when we left Limasol by night and landed in Port Said along with French troops. We landed on the beaches and moved cautiously into the city. There was no opposition, but that was to come four or five hours after we landed. Airborne troops had landed inland and our planes supported us as well, but for four or five days the fighting was quite intense.

World reaction led by America was hostile, and after occupying Port Said for three weeks we had to withdraw. It was really a forlorn expedition right from the beginning and with the benefit of hindsight, even if the Israeli-French-British push had been successful and the objectives well secured, the politicians of the world would have decided in Egypt's favour. As far as I was concerned it was an interesting adventure and I was able to test myself in my new rank and managed to cope reasonably well.

I returned to Cyprus by troopship and from there flew back to Catterick Camp in Yorkshire and then to Chester where I was finally demobbed after thirty-six years service, on 29 February 1957. I had in the course of that long period of time collected fifteen campaign medals, so I had a chestful of medals to show for my service to the country.

It was a strange feeling to be released from the army. I was very much conditioned to the life. It was an ordered life. To be a successful soldier you don't really have to have much initiative. The army thinks for you. I like to think that I did maintain my individuality throughout the years of service. I had seen a number of campaigns, some successful, some lost causes. I was, as it were, in at the death of the Empire. This was hard to take in some respects. Once India, the jewel of the Imperial Crown, went in 1947, country after country wanted to be free of the colonial power. I think that we got out of most countries, including India, reasonably gracefully. 'The old order changeth yielding place to new', and the change could at times be painful and bloody.

6 After the Army—What?

As I have said, soldiers are respected only in wartime. In peacetime, they are rather looked upon as a necessary evil and frankly I found peacetime soldiering boring and repetitive. I am not the stuff heroes are made of, but I did find that even in the civil disturbances in India, Cyprus and the Canal Zone, there was a spice of adventure which certainly added a different dimension to the soldier's life.

I was, of course, now faced with quite a problem: what to do with the remainder of my life? I had no desire to stay in England. I felt an alien there. I found the people insular, and full of self-interest, and the weather unbearable. I need the sun on my back and it can be as hot as it likes. I had no relatives, no ties to keep me in Britain. The big problem was that I was not really trained for any kind of profession. The army had been my life, and I knew nothing else. I had read a lot and I knew a fair bit of history and had a particular bias towards Middle Eastern affairs, but only as an interested amateur.

I had a feeling that I wanted to do something useful, something constructive, something that would be personally satisfying. My life as a soldier had been satisfying up to a point. I had seen fascinating, exotic places, and I had played my part in keeping law and order in various places, and had survived the horrors of the Burma-Siam Railway, but there was something missing. I had served as faithfully as I could, my monarch and my country, but now with the piece of my life that was left, I wanted to serve people, people in need. I had seen much suffering in my army days, suffering which was caused by man's inhumanity to man. I had also learned that the world is a small place and that although there may be differences due to culture, to religion and to colour, basically all men are the same, all are searching for happiness, and for peace of mind. I reckoned that I could find that precious

53

peace of mind by serving others for the rest of my life.

I had become fascinated by Mahatma Gandhi's life and philosophy. His negation of self, and his compulsive desire to serve his people, I found most moving. There was something Christlike about his personal simplicity and the simplicity of his philosophy. Christ and Gandhi both stressed that the most important commandments were to love God and your neighbour. I felt that through loving my neighbour, my neighbour in need, I could perhaps come to a better under-standing of God. I knew that I had to return to India. India was more home to me than Britain. I knew by this time I would like to do some kind of social work. I did not want any kind of salary as I had my army pension, and I knew that my wants were simple—a clean room, regular meals and that was about it. I knew even then that what I really wanted to emulate was the kind of commitment that a priest or a nun makes when he or she enters holy orders. I wanted the commitment without the discipline of the order. I had had my share of discipline in the army and I wanted to be able to rely on my own self-discipline to honour any kind of obligation I might make. If the truth were told I was a bit afraid of the future. At the moment of demobilisation I felt very much alone. I had no wife to go home to, no close friend to whom I could talk. In fact, I went to stay with my old batman and his family in the East End of London. He was a working man, but he took me in at a time when I really felt friendless. He and his family helped me

over that initial period of shock, when I discovered that I was a free agent and could make decisions for myself.

I decided that I would return home to India, that I would go by slow boat and I would read and relax and unwind. The cargo ship had fifteen passengers, mostly Burmese students returning from studying in London. It was a pleasant trip. Sadly, the Egyptian Authorities would not allow me to land in Egypt because my civilian passport had my occupation as 'retired army officer'.

I had a good time, however, in Khartoum and then after Aden we ran into the worst storm I have ever encountered. It was frightening in the extreme. The ship was like a cork in the seething black turmoil which was the sea. Two days and nights we were thrown hither and thither until we reached the shelter of the Western Indian coastline. We bypassed India and put into Rangoon. From Rangoon I made a nostalgic trip to Moulmein and looked up a few Burmese who had been kind to me during my stay there. There followed a holiday in one of the world's most exciting places, Hong Kong, then a few days in Singapore, and from there a Dutch steamer brought me to Calcutta.

I came to Calcutta for many reasons. I was fond of the city. During my various postings in Jabbalpur I had made many trips to it. In fact I had some luggage and boxes there which had been waiting for me for twenty years! I stayed at the Fairlawn Hotel. I suppose, if I am honest, I had always known I would end up in Calcutta. I think perhaps my Cook's Tour of the Far East was simply delaying the

Hong Kong market scene

inevitable. It was almost as if I felt I must
see as much of the world as possible
before submitting myself to a self-
imprisoned exile in this city. I had'a
feeling even then that I would never see
these places again which was strange
considering I was still comparatively
young. I have travelled widely but
nowhere have I seen such need as in
Calcutta. It has always been a problem
city. The fact that it has the highest
population density known anywhere does
not help the situation. The fact that it was
created on a swamp does not help. In
British times the servants of the company
died like flies of cholera and dysentery. It
is an unhealthy city. Amongst the
crumbling buildings in central Calcutta
can still be seen some fine examples of
Victorian buildings. Despite the lack of
paint they still have a kind of pathetic
grandeur.

The real slums are not really the seedy
unpainted tenements but the *bustees*.
These are acres of shacks, scattered
throughout the city and mixed up with
quite respectable areas. The *bustee* areas
have no amenities and the huts are made
of kerosene tins, bits of hessian, bamboo,
mud walls and, because of the insanitary
conditions, are real death-traps from a
health point of view. Statistics about
population, deaths, births are just
impossible to obtain for these areas. Even
the *bustee* dwellers are not at the bottom
of the social scale. There are estimated to
be about a million pavement-dwellers,
people who, incredibly, were born homeless and will eventually die homeless. A
million people, a staggering statistic, the

Crumbling buildings in central Calcutta

Housing development

Bustees

Slum alleyway. Cricket test match score is as newsworthy in India as in England

Professional beggars

Major Lesher of the Salvation Army, DG and Indian helper with camera-conscious youngsters

more staggering because the figure never improves, and never lessens. Calcutta grew unplanned. The city had a purpose: that was to make money for the East India Company, then for the nawabs and then for the Mogul Emperor in Delhi. Calcutta became the commercial capital of British India.

How could it happen? How could the Second City of the British Empire, inhabited by a people who are generally acknowledged to be very articulate, very politically-minded and in a strange ironical way socially conscious, how could this happen? All kinds of explanations can be produced: some economic, some geographic. Influxes of refugees are blamed. The truth perhaps is that the city began to die in British days. They kept the centre of the city clean and attractive because these were the areas they were using, but they obviously paid little attention to planning amenities for the areas they were not personally involved in. Now, the problems of the city have become so vast, so overpowering that even the most efficient and sophisticated government would find it difficult to unravel all the complications and all the social problems which now exist. One sometimes wishes that Calcutta could just disappear, and the city be resurrected somewhere else.

Pandit Nehru called Calcutta 'a Nightmare City'. Rather appropriately the patron deity of Calcutta is Kali, the Hindu goddess of death. Kali is a threatening goddess, a frightening goddess, and somehow death and despair are ever present in the endless struggle for

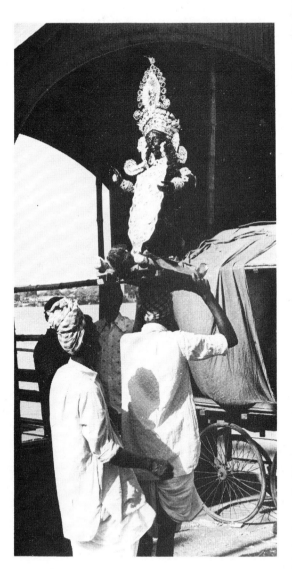

Statue of the Hindu goddess Kali

survival which is the lot of at least *two million* in the city. It is not that the government is impervious to the crying needs of this city. Far from it. Plans have been drawn up, money has been spent, but somehow against the vast backcloth of the problem the projects started seem very nominal and sadly do not seem to have excited any great civic response.

The sad fact is, of course, that although the great bulk of the citizens of Calcutta live a hand-to-mouth existence, a minority are extremely wealthy. It is really a rich city and in some ways a very cultured and exciting city. The European nabobs have been replaced by Marwari tycoons who live in elegant mansions in Alipore and Ballygunge and lead a life so very similar to the Europeans who previously owned the houses. The race course, the Polo Club, the Swimming Club, the Tollygunge Club and the Royal Golf Club are patronised as assiduously by the wealthy Indians as they were by the shopkeepers of the Raj. Just as their British predecessors with a few exceptions saw little of the real suffering Calcutta, so the Bengali or Marwari businessman is completely isolated by attitude from the squalor and degrading poverty around him.

Marxism flourishes in Calcutta for various reasons. The striking contrast between wealth and abject poverty must be a contributory factor. Festering ghettos must be a breeding ground for revolutionary ideas. Change comes slowly in India. And to young radicals, brought up themselves in ghetto conditions, it must appear that the 'old order' never changes and it must be tempting to think in terms

Temple dedicated to the goddess Kali

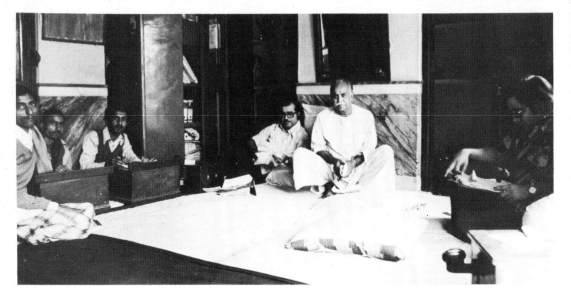

Marwari businessman

Elegant mansion of Alipore district

Calcutta race course

Mullick family's marble palace

of revolution as an antidote to the scars and hurts of degrading poverty. Yet even Marxist zeal cannot penetrate the enveloping blanket of apathy which covers the city. I find apathy a most irritating attitude. It is so absolutely negative and I feel that if only this wide-spread phenomenon could be changed, great changes could be wrought. When you consider the tremendous pool of cheap labour which is available, so much could be done by way of reconstruction. How irritating it is when the Monsoon rains deluge the city that inevitably the streets flood, because the drains are simply inadequate to cope with the volume of water! They have been inadequate for years and years and nothing is done to effect an improvement.

Calcutta is in some ways a sad city but nevertheless it is a city throbbing with life, full of surprises, full of movement and to me preferable to Delhi, which is impersonal, cold and unfriendly. As I said before, Calcutta assaults the senses. As you walk down any street in Calcutta all your senses are stimulated by the sights, the smells, the touch of seething humanity. I never feel alone in this city, not like the way one feels alone and lost in a European city. I always feel part of the vibrating life of Calcutta. I find after all these years I relate to her people. Calcutta, more than any other city east of Suez, was always awake to new ideas from the West. I don't think for a moment that a European can ever completely understand the Asian mind. I have perhaps got as near as is possible, because of the bizarre life I lead.

Communistic wall slogans

I like the Bengali. He tends to be voluble, excitable, arrogant, self-opinionated and emotional, but he makes a good friend. The Bengali does feel superior to most of the other communities. He considers himself cultured compared to some of the other communities. He considers, correctly, that Bengali literature is second to none, that Bengal is the centre of the Arts, that the Bengali film industry is superior to that of Bombay or Madras. He considers himself to be knowledgeable and politically aware, and a great number of Bengalis are steeped in the literature of the West. The Bengali coffee shops and tea-stalls are the places where world politics are discussed fervently and with knowledge. This makes the derelict state of the city all the more puzzling. The Bengali seems incapable of focusing his concern on his own backyard. His social consciousness, which is usually clothed in political terms, is obviously more theoretical than practical. If you discuss the state of the city with an articulate Bengali, he will agree with you, shrug his shoulders, spread his hands expressively and say 'What to do!' and then go on to discuss the latest peace-move in the Middle East, or his views on the proliferation of nuclear arms. I suppose, in all fairness to him, he has simply come to terms with the awful helplessness that anyone feels in looking objectively at the problems of the city.

I am in one sense immune to human suffering. I have seen so much of it. If I let myself become emotional about the folk I feed, I could never cope. It is not that I am

Bengali woman

any harder than on my first visit to the city. It is rather that I have developed a defence mechanism which is essential for survival. Hard work and total concentration on what I am doing has helped in a way to blunt the disturbing effect of living in a city where hundreds of thousands find it hard to live. I can, however, still be moved, even to tears, by the sight of young children or old people suffering. They seem so tragically vulnerable, those at either end of the age scale.

For months prior to coming to Calcutta I had known that I wanted to find a social work type of job. I had served thirty-six years in the army and I am proud of my period of service. I felt, however, that although I had seen a great deal, suffered considerably and had had a reasonably satisfying career in the army, there was something lacking. During my military career I had seen people suffering; very often the innocent suffer much more than the military in modern warfare. I decided then that as I was a comparatively young man and fit I would try to do a further thirty-six years serving the poor people. I have completed twenty years, so I have sixteen years to go.

About this time I was offered a job in the Dr Graham's Homes, Kalimpong, as a housefather. I was tempted to escape to the cool of the hills to beautiful Kalimpong, but declined. I felt the Calcutta situation was more pressing. I also toyed with the idea of helping with the Tibetan refugee problems. I had always been fascinated by Tibet. It has an attractive aura of mystery for me. I felt a great sympathy for the Tibetans who had fled before the Chinese advance through their country, and had gone over the high passes into North Eastern India. Again, however, as I walked round the Calcutta back streets I felt very strongly that this was where I could perhaps do most good. I began to feel that a job in Kalimpong or in a Tibetan refugee camp in Darjeeling was just an escape from a responsibility which some unseen power was calling me to fulfil.

Did God call me to work in Calcutta? I have always rejected this idea because I felt that my humble contribution was not really worthy of his notice, of his consideration. My life up to the point of my arrival in Calcutta had been singularly lacking in spiritual depth. Through daily contact with suffering, however, I have become more aware of God's presence.

Having said that, I should add that I do not see anything ennobling in suffering. I have in Calcutta, during my twenty years of service to the poor, seen every possible degree of suffering amongst my large dependent family. No! suffering in my view does not generally ennoble. In fact it so often does the opposite. A starving person will do anything to obtain food. I saw this in the prison camp, I have seen it in the Middle East, and I have seen it in Calcutta. Hunger is such a compulsive need. Where you have abject poverty what we would consider to be civilised values disappear and there is a return to jungle law: the strong survive. I do not believe that God makes people suffer either as a punishment, or as a means of purifying them. Hunger is too basic and too debasing to be a purifying influence.

If a man is dying of hunger can he really be blamed if he steals to stay alive? The instinct to survive is an equally strong motivation.

My relationship with God is something which has been growing with the years. Very often, I must confess, I question what kind of God it is who would permit such suffering and misery. This questioning is only on my black days, when I have perhaps come across some particular tragedy, probably involving the death of some child. I hate to see children suffer. Dull, glazed eyes and the swollen stomach, symptoms of acute malnutrition, never fail to move me. Why does God let children suffer? I doubt if the most learned theologian can really give an adequate answer to that most probing of questions.

I am a Protestant and a member of a church here in Calcutta, but I seldom go to church as my feeding programme includes Sunday. God said, 'Six days shalt thou labour and on the seventh rest.' Good, but unfortunately people also require to eat on the seventh day and one of the necessary features of any feeding programme of this type is that it is a seven-days-a-week programme. As I have grown older, and I hope a little wiser, I have become more and more conscious of the need for a deeper belief as a means of recharging my batteries. Often at night I speak to God in prayer and ask his help with some pressing problem. It has taken me a long time to reach this point of contact and I would not say that I am convinced that I am on the hot-line direct to heaven. I read my Bible reasonably regularly and apart from the spiritual truths which it contains I love the sound of the language. When I am really depressed, tired or sick I turn to *1 Corinthians 13* and read the passage about 'love', and I feel refreshed and encouraged. I have to confess at times I suffer from acute depression bordering, sometimes, on melancholia. These moods of darkness, which cause me to be very irritable and impatient with my workers are sadly becoming more frequent as I get older. I think the moods are due to a combination of loneliness, and the lack of a sincere friend to whom I can pour out my troubles. True, I speak to God at times, but I'm never fully convinced that he is listening. I must say I envy people like Mother Teresa who have no doubts, who have an absolute certainty that God is a person with whom the closest relationship is possible. At times I feel this.

My attitude to God is rather Hindu. I go to God who is holy but whose message is too lofty to understand. I prefer my path to enlightenment to be gradual, a growing in the faith, if you like. I am a bit sceptical of the lightning conversions, the sudden decisions of absolute commitment to God. If I had had such a conversion, I think I would find the weight of guilt unbearable, as I inevitably failed to measure up to the standard I imagined God wanted of me. No, I think God accepts me as I am with all my failings and with all my doubts.

Calcutta Cathedral—DG's church

7 Calcutta Claims Me

So I selected Calcutta to be my base for some kind of social work or, perhaps, more accurately, Calcutta selected me.

I remembered from previous visits to the city during wartime the kindness of the Salvation Army who ran canteens and hostels for troops on leave. Any serving soldier, sailor or airman has a warm spot for the Salvation Army. Their canteens were always near the troubled areas and their charity was always dispensed with a cheerful smile and an encouraging word. I was very surprised to find that Captain Don Smith, who had run the Red Shield Canteen in war-time, was still in Calcutta and he gave me a warm welcome, as did Major Barbara Powell who was Secretary to the Territorial Commander then on leave. I informed Don Smith that I wanted to do some kind of social work and that I was not interested in remuneration but would like a roof over my head and some food. He sent me with a note down to the Salvation Army Social Service Centre in Lower Circular Road to report to Captain Robert E Bath, who was planning to run a feeding programme.

I found the Centre with considerable difficulty. It is tucked away up a narrow lane not too far from Sealdah Station and interestingly enough almost directly opposite the Mother House of Mother Teresa's Missionaries of Charity. Lower Circular Road at one time housed the affluent city merchants. Now it throbs with life and is one of the main arteries of this city which never sleeps. The tram-cars, swamped with people, clang along the busy thoroughfares, and all kinds of shops do business there. On one side of the street the shops tend to be temporary wooden structures selling plastic goods, holy pictures, basket work, furniture, earthenware jars. The road is filled with holes and the taxis and cars swerve madly to avoid jolting their passengers too badly. It is a noisy street, the traffic sounds mingle with the bleat of the hawkers and

Aerial view of Calcutta

Maidan area of Calcutta

Trams on Lower Circular Road

Crowded station forecourt

Pavement bookstall

Cows, which Hinduism looks upon as holy, meander along street and pavement

Holy pictures on sale

Protected animal takes her rest

the shouts of the naked children who swarm everywhere. Holy cows meander solemnly through the masses of people and stray dogs, nuzzling into the garbage heaps looking for morsels to eat. It is almost with a sense of relief that one turns off Lower Circular Road into the quiet lane and into the Headquarters of the Salvation Army Social Service Centre.

Captain Robert E Bath received me kindly enough, but questioned me very closely. It was natural that he should be suspicious of this character who had turned up out of the blue and who was very vague as to what he actually wanted to do. I suppose it was a bit odd too, for an ex-military officer, to be willing to work for only his keep, and yet not suggest that God had called him to work amongst the poor and needy. The Captain certainly grilled me, but I obviously satisfied him about my sincerity. In fact he lost no time in putting me to the test. I expect he thought that I would soon lose interest in the unglamorous job he envisaged for me.

He took me to a corner of a rather depressing courtyard where there was an old kitchen area. He showed me where wood and coke were stored and gave me some cooking utensils. He informed me he would supply me with food, and that after I had cooked it he would give me the use of a small car and I would go into the city and distribute the food. It all sounded very easy in theory. He did give me a bit of a sermon, in that he added that people eat seven days a week, and if I agreed to take on this commitment, I would have to realise that I would be committed to this programme seven days a week. I have been true to this commitment for twenty years.

I shall ever be grateful to the Salvation Army for taking me in and launching my feeding programme. I think that first day in the courtyard, I suffered a bit from an anticlimax. I had in my plans for doing social work seen myself as a large, male version of Florence Nightingale flitting through the slums and the *bustee* areas bringing light and hope to the mass of poor. The Salvation Army people are generally matter-of-fact folk. The nature of their service makes them this way. They see people as they are, in the raw as it were, and therefore they have no need for pretence; they say what they mean without fuss and without beating about the bush. That first day, therefore, when my duties were pointed out to me was a kind of anticlimax. It was obvious that this was to be no glamorous job. My feeding programme was not going to be launched with a roll of drums and a host of grateful people shaking my hand and wishing me well. I don't know quite what I expected. Did I expect a little more fuss to be made of me? If I did, I was to be disappointed. As I have said, I think the sincerity of my commitment was doubted, and I cannot blame the Salvation Army for being a bit doubtful about an ex-professional soldier who had drifted round the world and who unexpectedly turned up on their Calcutta door step.

The good Captain showed me the room which has been my home for twenty years. Naturally, over the years I have added bits and pieces to it and now it is really quite comfortable. It is small, and

twenty years ago when I first saw it, it looked very much like a monk's cell. It had the bare necessities: bed, wardrobe and dressing table, and that was it! The view was hardly inspiring, looking out on to the busy courtyard but, at least it was what I had asked for—a roof over my head, and it has become over the years my haven, my refuge from the noise, bustle, and pressures of living. I rarely invite anyone to my room. This is not because I am ashamed of it, but because I feel the need of somewhere to retreat to—somewhere I can be completely alone, where I can unwind and be with my own thoughts. My room is a refuge from the outside world.

DG's room—'home' for more than 20 years

Captain Bath of the Salvation Army
Don Smith

Gateway to the Salvation Army's Social Service Centre

The courtyard below DG's room

Early days. Major Lesher, DG and three helpers at the Centre soon after its opening (early sixties)

The feeding programme started off on a very small scale. We had a list of fifty-five people, shut-ins, sick and old people who without our help would have perished. I used to cook food for them every day and take it out in tiffin carriers to these folk and bring back the previous day's carrier. In addition about one hundred and twenty to one hundred and thirty people used to come to the Centre at lunchtime and sit at wooden tables in a corner of the courtyard; we fed them seven days a week. It was all very cosy and very neatly organised. It was tempting to keep the programme to such manageable proportions.

My trip to the shut-ins took about an hour as most of them were in a single area, close to the Centre. I did, however, by this simple beginning, become more and more aware of the immensity of the problem. Some of the shut-ins lived by themselves in one-room hovels. The stench in some of them was unbelievable. Some of them were Anglo-Indians who had fallen on really bad days. A number of them were old, whose families had emigrated and just left them and departed from India to make a new life for themselves in Britain or Australia. I find this kind of situation not only touching but annoying. The Anglo-Indian community has many weaknesses, as do all communities, but their treatment of old people sometimes leaves much to be desired. Normally in Indian families old age is respected and even revered, but the number of elderly, destitute Anglo-Indians I have helped to feed in the last twenty years suggests that certain

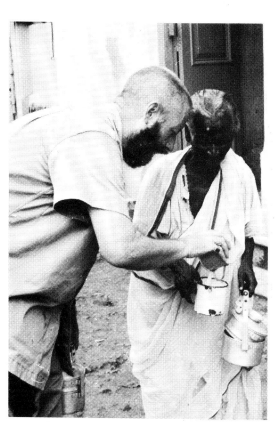

A drink for an old lady

members of the community are careless of their responsibilities to the old. The elderly sick Anglo-Indians were of course nominally Christian, Protestant and Roman Catholic. It should be stressed that we made no distinction on a religious basis right from those early days. We never have categorised people as 'Christian', 'Hindu' or 'Muslim'. They are simply people who are hungry. It is interesting that now we are feeding over six thousand daily; it works out that roughly about one third are Hindu, one third Muslim and one third Christian. It just happens this way.

I think, however, if I am being very honest, that the plight of the Anglo-Indian community in Calcutta has caused me more concern than the plight of Hindus or Muslims. I suppose, in a way, I am really Anglo-Indian myself, having spent so long in the country, and I suppose I feel a certain responsibility to this community which has been left behind. It was *created* by the British and, to a certain extent, *used* by the British—and in a way *deserted* by the British.

It is now a community largely without a middle class. There has been massive emigration by those who could afford the fares and who had some kind of profession or skill to offer the receiving country. The poor of the community have been left behind. Calcutta has always attracted the less worthy of the community. Even in the days of the Raj, there were large numbers of Anglo-Indian derelicts to be found in the city, more than in any other city. So many Anglo-Indians who are left still find it

DG greets a mother with baby and little boy

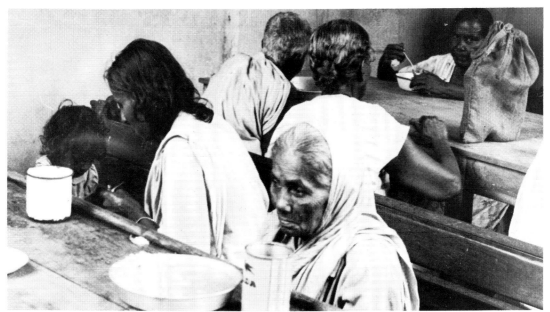

Young and old people attend the Social Service Centre for daily meal

DG, back to camera, opens up food van

Captain Don Smith midst happy crowd of children

Robert + Bath

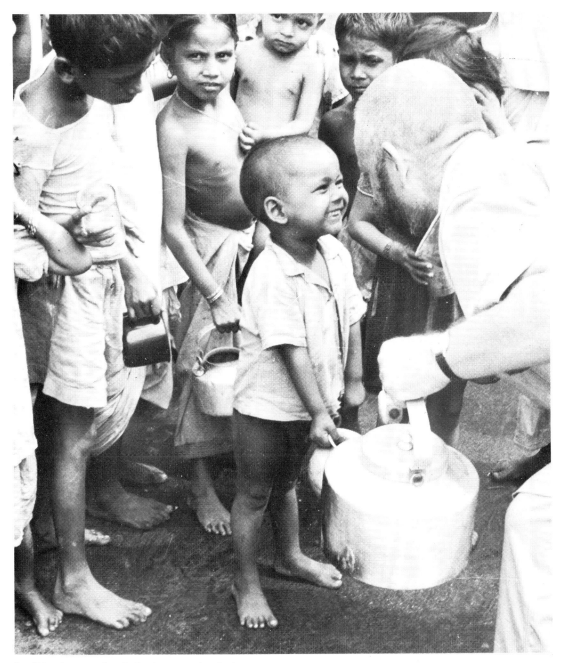

Small boy has special smile for the man with a kettle

very difficult to integrate. They still cling to the customs, the values, the outlook of the British of yesteryear. They yearn for a day that has long gone. They dream of escaping from their poverty and from their problems by going to the United Kingdom or Australia, where, they imagine (oh so wrongly!) that all their problems would be solved, and everyone would accept them and be kind. They dream, too, of what they consider a happier past where, under the British, they held a kind of privileged position. Many of them are unskilled and have little to offer a prospective employer. Sadly, there are a great number of illiterate young Anglo-Indians and this is a new phenomenon. The community was justifiably proud of the fact that it was the only community in India that was one hundred per cent literate. Now there are scores of young Anglo-Indians who do not attend Anglo-Indian Schools and live on their wits in the back streets. The fees of the Anglo-Indian Schools are quite high and many of them feel strongly that they should pay lower fees in what, they consider, are their own schools.

These schools, however, if they are to maintain their high standards, have to charge realistic fees to cover their costs. The Anglo-Indian parents do not help by constantly talking about better times in the past. These unemployed and largely unemployable youngsters cause me great heartache. They seem to have no loyalties. They are footloose and all they seem interested in is western 'pop' music and going to the cinema. They are constantly begging from people, constantly

borrowing money, constantly in debt and as a result they live off their parents, contributing nothing for their keep. Many of them are delinquent and end up in trouble with the police. The Anglo-Indian girls seem to fare better. They make excellent typists and secretaries and are in great demand by the commercial firms in the city. The girls earn very good wages, and so another problem arises in that the female in a household often can earn as much as three times more than the male who is doing an unskilled job. This situation is an explosive one and does not make for happy family relations. If Anglo-Indians would only regulate their living standards, and their expenses to something like the Indian standards, they could cope much better. My Bengali helpers here live on about five rupees per day; Anglo-Indians would expect ten or twenty. It is yet again the old problem of non-adaption to circumstances and to reality.

Anglo-Indian leaders and politicians like Frank Anthony have done a good job in trying to develop a pride in the community. It has not been an easy task as most of the community with initiative and drive have tended to leave. Some Anglo-Indians have made good and realised, I think quite correctly, that they are better off in India than overseas, where they tend to be always that bit different and apart from the local people.

The mixed-blood community suffers perhaps most from the inability to come to terms psychologically with their situation. In all fairness to them, and with their difficulties about employment and

Mealtime at the Social Service Centre

with the Indians rather suspicious about the community which appears to have divided loyalties, it is not surprising that the Anglo-Indians who are left give the appearance of opting out of even trying to make a niche for themselves in India. Anglo-Indians have always been improvident, tending to live for the present and content to let the future take care of itself. Those who do make good and have become integrated, are a very talented group, and are capable of imaginative thinking; many have made their mark not only in India but internationally as well.

It is ironical that one of the main points which critics of immigration make in the United Kingdom is that the Indian and Pakistani immigrant often makes little attempt to integrate into the British way of life when one considers how that, in India, they believe they already follow that lifestyle!

Even in the early days of the feeding programme when I came across Anglo-Indians in difficulties I did my best to help them. Some of the older men and women I would try to get into old folks' homes where they would be cared for.

I suppose colonialism brought some benefits to the emerging countries but it also took a terrible toll in terms of human misery and despair. The mixed-blood community with its many problems is a legacy of the Raj which concerns any sensitive British person who knows the situation and who can reject the white-faced superiority which so often colours his attitude to India and Indians. Having said that, however, I become irritated with

so many Anglo-Indians who are content to carry on begging and do so little to help themselves. They pester me for their rent, for money for medical help, money for food and money for school fees for their children. The demands they make are never ending and it is impossible for me to help in all these areas. There is a certain decadence in a proportion of the community which is sad, as they seem incapable of self help.

This decadence is, of course, not confined only to the Anglo-Indian community. Far from it. One of my main tasks, and it is a gargantuan one, is with the help of my one social worker, trying to ensure that the people on my feeding-list deserve to be there, and are not just loafers or spongers who could find work if they would be bothered. The city is full of hangers-on, who would be prepared to live on charity for the rest of their days if they could get away with it. This is why I have instituted careful checks on my 'clients' right from the beginning of my feeding programme. To begin with I was naive and I'm sure some plausible rascals conned me quite easily. Twenty years later, I am not too easily duped and I would like to think that the vast majority of my folk are really deserving. We make it clear that we are not contemplating feeding them for ever and a day, but that in their difficult circumstances, which we hope will be temporary, we will tide them over until conditions improve for them. This applies more to the young than the elderly.

Mrs Hossein, my social worker, assesses those on the feeding programme every

On the food run, saucepan is the best ladle

three months, and a year is the limit a
person can be on the programme. If,
however, after that period there is no
betterment in the person's situation and
Mrs Hossein feels that there has been a
real attempt made by the person to look
for work then, obviously, we are not just
going to let the person starve to death and
we reinstate him or her for a further
period on the programme.

One of the delights of doing social work
in Calcutta is that there is no religious
segregation at all. The problems are so
immense that in the face of them there is
great cohesion amongst all organisations
trying to tackle the vast problems. First of
all there are no barriers between the
various Christian organisations at work in
the city. The Roman Catholics are the
most numerous of the Christians. They do
not adopt any exclusive attitudes,
however, and relations with them are
good. I find they are essentially practical
in their programmes, and they have a very
charitable attitude to human failings. I
always find this strange considering what
these priests and nuns have given up
because of their commitment to their
faith. If I come across any derelict with
whom I feel cannot cope even with food
provided daily, I pass him to Mother
Teresa, who has never refused to take
anyone I have sent. She trusts my
judgement, and I appreciate this and
respond to this trust by not burdening her
with the care of someone about whom I
have doubts.

I help her with medicine and she often
helps me with supplies of food like
bulghur wheat. We have the happiest

*DG with sack of sweets for children of the inmates of the
Home for Dying Destitutes, which is run by Mother Teresa*

working relationship, realising that we are both really doing the same job by different methods. In the early days of the feeding programme I helped Mother Teresa by taking food to her home for the dying destitutes in Kalighat. Into this Home she brought the dying men and women destitutes in that city, those often found lying in the alleys and streets. There they at least died with dignity. In Nirmal Hriday is to be seen the real evidence of what malnutrition can do to a person. In Mother's eyes, however, they are God's children. Some, of course, recover. I find the Home, after countless visits, inspirational, for it is to my mind one of the purest pieces of Christian work I have ever witnessed. The nurses of the Order quietly and efficiently wash the patients, talk to them, soothe them, feed them and if they do die, they die knowing some kindness and perhaps with some peace of mind. I no longer go there to feed the hundred people in the Home. As my programme grew, I just could not cope with going. And as Mother's work became well known she did not need my assistance.

The Anglican cathedral in Calcutta is responsible for some very imaginative social work. The late Canon Subir Biswas took a relatively staid and complacent congregation and made it aware of the great need all around, and then made it aware of its own potential for concern. Many of the congregation became conscious of the great reservoirs of concern within them, which they did not know existed until Canon Biswas involved them in some of the work of the

Mother Teresa and Canon Subir Biswas

Kalikatta Bustee Pralati Sangstha, known for convenience as KBPS. The aim of this association, which co-ordinates voluntary agencies belonging to various Churches, is a very realistic one. It is to bring to the *bustee* area planning for better sanitation: one lavatory for twenty-five people, one tap for fifty people, education, and above all some semblance of civic pride. It is a realistic programme because it realises that the hope of rehousing two and a half million is a vain one, and therefore the KBPS seeks to improve the *bustees* themselves. It tries to combat the apathy which pervades the *bustee* areas. The programme of advancement and improvement has been set up to be the servant and not the master of the *bustee* people and their changing situation. Canon Biswas's premature death was a sad blow for Calcutta. He had boundless energy and the ability to inspire people to self-examination, and in many cases to inspire them to look beyond their self-interest, to become involved in the great morass of despair which is such a large part of the Calcutta scene.

My own work is more individual. I have been a long time in the field and, although I have lots of good friends and contacts amongst the agencies helping Calcutta, I tend to work on my own, although under the aegis of the Salvation Army. This suits my nature and because of my own total involvement, it allows me to keep my ancillary staff to a reasonable number. I have discovered the golden rule in dealing with staff: have as few as possible so that they haven't time to grumble and make each other discontented!

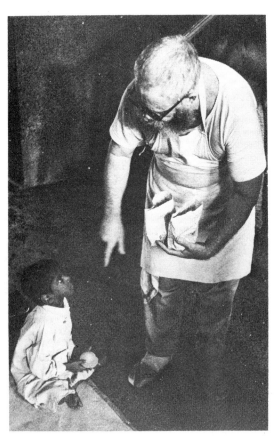

Child in Mother Teresa's Home receives sweets from DG

Canon Biswas sitting in a Land Rover sent to him by Christian Aid, Calcutta Cathedral in background

Four members of DG's staff

My staff in the Centre consists of five drivers and six kitchen workers. I could not manage with any less as each man has to have a day off. They give good service, but require constant supervision.

There are also Hindu and Muslim societies doing good work in the city. They don't receive much publicity because they tend to be formed by people of a certain type who work exclusively for the members of their own community. Neither the Hindu religion nor the Muslim religion have the caring outreach of Christianity, although there are some exceptions to this. The Sikhs, for example, use their temples as social centres, and any Sikh in trouble or difficulty can expect to find assistance there. It is a proud boast of the Sikhs that one never sees a Sikh begging, and this is absolutely true.

I am aware that the work I do does not cure the problems of the city. My work is not preventive by any manner of means. I am, however, as realistic as the KBPS. I could do nothing to improve the general lot of the slum-, or the *bustee-*, or the pavement-dweller. Their lot has defied the efforts of more sophisticated organisations than mine. I simply help to keep them alive.

Cynics ask, 'why bother?' 'If their only means of keeping alive is a free meal given by you each day, what is the point of prolonging their existence which is a far from happy one?' 'Would they not be better dead for all that life has to offer them, and if they did die there would be fewer mouths to feed and more food to go round?' I have actually been asked these questions. My answer to people who

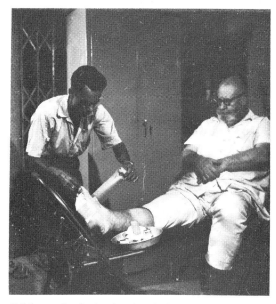

DG having his feet bandaged, a daily operation

think this way is that human life is precious and should be sustained and nurtured as far as possible. In the jungle the weak require to be protected, so it is in life. It is one of God's wishes that we help and sustain our weaker brothers and sisters. My feeding programme has very often helped people over a sticky period and after a time they have managed to obtain jobs and their fortunes have changed. As I say, my aim is very basic, keeping the people on my programme alive. I am content with this limited but essential goal. I think I have survived because I have not seen myself as a crusading reformer railing against the social ills and demanding from politicians and the public in general better living conditions for my clients. I haven't time to do this, and I am not gifted enough to eloquently express their case. I know that really I would be asking for the impossible, so I am content to answer and satisfy man's basic need—hunger. At least in the early days of my feeding programme this is all I did.

The Salvation Army discovered eventually that my dedication to my task was not a passing fad, but that I was prepared to put down roots and stay put. I am a civilian worker for the Salvation Army. Everything I do, as it were, I do under the banner of the Salvation Army. I have not shirked my duty. I have kept reasonable health although neglected varicose veins have become badly infected and require constant dressing. At times too I become tired, largely because of the nagging pains in my legs, particularly in very hot weather.

8 The Daily Round

I get up very early in the morning and, in fact, exist on very little sleep—five to six hours at the most. When I do sleep I sleep very deeply and it takes a great disturbance to rouse me from this sleep. Unlike most people who have lived a long time in the East I retire to bed late—between 12 and 1.30 am.

Having a beard is a great advantage in that I don't have to shave!

Early morning in Calcutta is a pleasant time. It is cool, and one wakens to the cawing of the Calcutta crows greeting a new day. Crows are not my favourite birds, but they have a cheeky persistence and somehow their noisy chatter is very much part of the Calcutta scene. Out in the courtyard some of my helpers wash under a tap and the horrible dawn-chorus of clearing their throats and spitting even after all these years almost succeeds in putting me off my breakfast.

The trams start clanging their way down Lower Circular Road and the varying smells from morning meals cooked over thousands of individual fires comes wafting up to my room. In the early morning at certain times of the year a pall of smog caused by the dung fires hangs over the city. The city never completely sleeps but by 7 am everyone is up and about his business, including the pavement-dwellers. I suppose they too are conditioned to their way of life. Many have known nothing but the pavement and have never known what it is to live in a house and, perhaps like the gipsies of Europe, a house or even a modest hut, might not be appreciated. Four walls might seem like a cage. I have tried to find the answer to this question, but one is met with the resigned shrug of the shoulders which does not really throw any light on the problem, or give a satisfactory answer.

I am usually up and washed and ready for work by the time the Institute bell rings signifying the start of the day's

Morning scene. Loaded vendors

Morning scene. Salesgirls

Another morning scene

Woman collecting cow dung for use as fuel. This practice deprives land of much-needed fertiliser

work. Everything is regulated to the sound of bells, because a number of workers don't have watches and so bells are necessary to signify tea and meal breaks. My staff are usually waiting for me outside the large dining room which measures sixty feet by twenty feet and when I unlock the door we prepare for the arrival of the vegetable contractors. In the early days of the programme I had to go to the market myself to purchase the fresh vegetables, but since the order is now large the Bengali contractor comes to me. I change the contractor quite frequently as I have found from past experience this is the only way to keep the vegetables up to a nutritious standard. An entrenched contractor soon starts to pass off rubbish, and you find that in the bulk order there are nice fresh greens on the top and rather weary bedraggled looking vegetables underneath. It is now known in the vegetable market that as soon as I find this kind of sharp practice happening I change the contractor.

The next half-hour is spent weighing the vegetables, and after the quite lengthy and monotonous operation is completed (about 7.30 am) the preparation of the vegetables begins and this takes my staff until about 9.45 am. During this time I sit at one of the dining room tables and do my administration work, checking the number of people I fed the day previously, doing my accounts and keeping the books in order. I have a tidy mind, and I must say I quite enjoy this period of the day. My book-keeping is comparatively simple and as the years have gone by what initially I regarded as something of a

necessary evil I now quite enjoy. While I
am doing this, I am often interrupted by
visitors arriving. I have visitors to the
Centre from all over the world. Kind
friends, including newspapermen and
those connected with television, have
made my work known throughout the
world, and people come to see for themselves this extraordinary chap who weighs
about twenty stones, who wears a rather
incongruous cloth cap, and wears only
white cotton trousers and a vast vest
stretched over a too large torso! Add a
large beard, reddish tinged with grey, and
also the fact that because of acute ulcers
on the legs and feet he can only wear
chappels and you have a bit of an oddity.
I hasten to add that there is nothing
gimmicky about my garb. I dress for
comfort and ease of movement in what is
one of the most exacting climates in the
world. I most warmly welcome all visitors
because, if they are intrigued by this
oddity and his strange work, they can be
generous. . . .

My sponsors come from all over the
world. *Help the Aged* continues to
support me. *The Unitarian Service
Committee of Canada* based in Ottawa
sponsored me generously for seven years
and then phased their help out over a
two-year period. *Oxfam* have helped
through the years. They gave me two
vehicles and help me with publicity. At
one time they used to help me financially,
but it is part of their policy, which I fully
understand and accept, that they give
support for a limited period only; they
believe that the people of the Third World
should be taught to support themselves.

DG at his book-keeping

DG and helper dealing with the paperwork which is all part of his scheme to bring food to the poor of Calcutta

My programme does not really fall into this category, but by limiting the time a person is on my programme I have, I hope, established a satisfactory compromise.

Oxfam supported me from 1960 and with their help the number fed jumped dramatically from fifty-five to two thousand. This was the kind of support I needed at that time. It gave a tremendous impetus to my work and I shall always be grateful to them for this timely boost.

The West German organisation *Brot für der Welt* took over from the Canadian Unitarian Organisation and has been generous in the extreme. It is very well organised and my project had to be thoroughly scrutinised before they would accept me on to the Asian Programme.

As I have been in this job for twenty years I understand that people cannot continue to sponsor for a period of that length, so I am aware that very often when an organisation sponsors me, it can only be for a limited time. If I run short of food at any time Mother Teresa always helps me out. It is very gratifying to know this.

The feeding programme costs four hundred thousand rupees a year to run and I am indebted to a number of kind folk throughout the world who help me keep going.

I receive marvellous regular support from the Church of Our Lady of the Wayside in Shirley, Warwickshire. Father Patrick O'Mahony, the parish priest, heads up this work, which—as with so many of my loyal and self-sacrificing supporters—could do with a chapter all by itself. Every week not less than £250 is sent for the feeding programme (Lloyds Bank kindly waive all charges for this service), on top of which further gifts of both money and materials for the medical and educational programmes are also sent.* One of the very important tasks Fr O'Mahony does on my behalf is to make himself available for crisis situations, in the most recent of which—the Calcutta floods—his exertions saved many thousands from death from a variety of causes such as exposure, starvation, snake bite and so on.

A gentleman called Frank Carter from Leatherhead in Surrey is another tremendous fund-raiser for my work. My association with him goes back to the early 'sixties. He was Oxfam's special representative between 1964-71, but has continued to serve in many ways (sacrificially, as always) since his retirement.

In Australia The Salvation Army, notably through the Bentley Corps, but by no means exclusively so, also make possible the continuance and expansion of my work.

Many various churches assist, too. As with another list of God's warriors, 'what more should I say?' for time would fail me to tell of all of them, and of the thousands of acts of generosity and thoughtfulness which lie behind their many actions. Folk like Wesley Gould and Major John Smith help me in Melbourne and Cecilia Prentice does a similar job in Sydney.

* This is further outlined in Father O'Mahony's important and recent book *The Fantasy of Human Rights* (Mayhew-McCrimmon, 1978, p 43).

One of the vehicles belonging to the Salvation Army

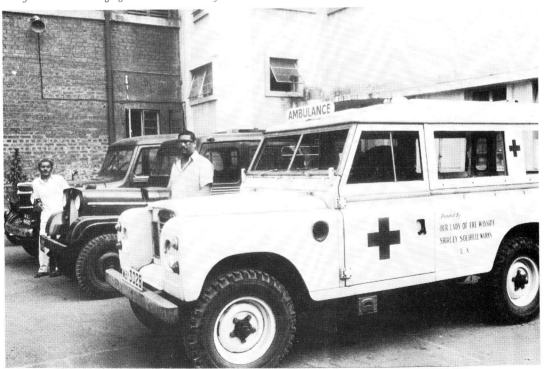

Some of the vehicles which have been donated to the Centre

In New Zealand, an organisation called CORSO from time to time helps me with medicine and food. A great deal of help has come from individuals, some of whom have seen for themselves what I am doing and others who have simply heard, or read.

The BBC did a documentary on me for the 'Man Alive' Programme which raised a good deal of interest in the United Kingdom. I never saw the film, of course, but from the donations which came to me I imagine it was quite a telling piece of work. I gather that one of the young boys whom I help, Asgar Ali, stole the show. He is now in Grade 9 at St James School and his reports are quite excellent, you will be glad to know!

I have therefore met some interesting people. David Frost came to see me some years ago, and I had never heard of him. I think he was impressed by that! I found him a person with a deep concern and Calcutta had obviously disturbed him deeply as it would any sensitive artist. He wrote an article on me and from the money which this article brought in I was able to purchase a Land Rover. This was done without any fanfare of publicity. So many celebrities want their good deeds to be highlighted as it is good for their public image. He came on my food-round with me and I found him to be interested and moved by the experience.

The day's work really consists of a series of monotonous chores. There is no glamour about the work whatsoever. Our cooking is to no *cordon bleu* standard, it could not be simpler. The first chore is to wash and prepare the vast amount of

Supervising the cooking

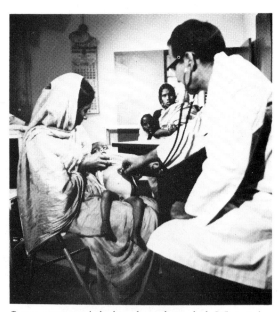

Doctor examining baby brought to clinic which DG started about 14 years ago. The project is funded directly by money coming from abroad

Mothers and children queueing for clinic

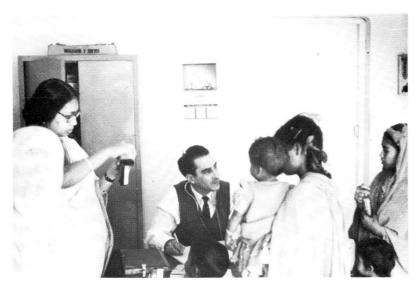

Dr John, Nurse Dass and patients at the Clinic. Note young Muslim girl on right, burqua *thrown over her head while in the consulting room*

vegetables we need for each day. In the old days the cooking was done in large cauldrons outside in the yard over wood fires. Now, we are much more sophisticated in that we have five gas rings in our quite modern kitchen next to the dining room. But it is a theoretic sophistication: very often no gas comes, and we have to revert to the older but more reliable method. Cooking outside in the Monsoon rain was an unpleasant and difficult job, but now we can cope quite adequately in all weathers. I supervise the cooking myself. I always have done so. I thus satisfy myself that the food is being cooked properly and not being wasted by careless handling or cooking. I suppose someone else should do this, but old customs die hard. In fairness to my staff my supervision has become more and more perfunctory as the years have gone by, and now consists of a long distance glance from the dining room table. The fact that I am there, however, is important. I am not, however, sitting idle for I keep very careful accounts which I render to the Salvation Army. No money is wasted and I am the only one of the team who handles money.

At this time, too, I have my breakfast, which consists of perhaps two eggs, toast and some puris, washed down by a bottle of ginger beer. My diet is of the simplest and I haven't really time for niceties.

A doctor and a nurse run a clinic from 7 am to 10 am in the room beside the kitchen. I started this work twelve years ago. I felt helpless that so many of my clients were suffering from all kinds of diseases and had no hope of being able to afford the simplest medicines, never

mind proper medical attention. It seemed to me, and I must confess it took me some time to want to take on a further responsibility, that there was not much point feeding people to keep them alive, if they were going to perish from disease which could be halted or even cured by some medication. Initially I was cautious about launching this project, because I wanted as always to be certain that I could continue the service and that it would not be just another project which petered out because of lack of money or interest. Dr John, an Armenian, is my full-time doctor and he is assisted by Mrs Dass, a Bengali Christian nurse. This medical project is not funded by the Salvation Army; I am responsible for raising the money for salaries and medicine myself, which I do with money coming from abroad. I would say that apart from dealing with the sick, we are more and more entering the field of preventive medicine. We send a large number of patients for X-ray screening. Dr Mukherjee, a fine Christian doctor, screens anyone we send to his clinic for eleven rupees, which is a very generous reduction of his normal fees. The doctor and the nurse try their best by talking to the patients to encourage them to consider hygiene, and we dispense vast quantities of vitamin pills to assist the well-being of the patients. Health education is one of the great needs of the country as a whole.

One of my dreams for the future is to be able to build a fifty-bed hospital. A kind friend has given me a plot of land in the Howrah district which would be an admirable site for such a project.

Howrah bridge

Howrah station

Unfortunately, to build such a hospital and adequately equip it would cost £100,000 which is a tremendous amount of money. I would envisage such a hospital caring mainly for patients suffering from tuberculosis, which is rife in the city because of the dampness and lack of nutritious food. A hospital is needed because TB requires long-term care. In India if a member of the family is hospitalised the family very often move in as well. So often our doctor prescribes streptomycin for patients with tuber-culosis but because of the cramped living conditions and the poor food, the drug does not really have a chance to be as effective as it might be.

It soon became obvious that a fixed location clinic was not enough. Many of the people in the food programme came from a distance, and since I had originally developed a mobile feeding service it seemed logical that a mobile dispensary should do a similar service. As you can imagine, I could do with a fleet of mobile clinics to be able to even scratch the surface of the problem. However, our one mobile clinic does a good job. It covers an area of thirty-five miles daily, except on Sunday when Dr John has his day off. All kinds of disease, complaints and injuries are dealt with. As we have become a little more solvent we hospitalise cases which require more intensive treatment than can be given in the clinic. We *pay* for this treatment for no treatment is free in India, just as no education is free. I have a worker whose special job is to keep a check on the needs of our folk in hospital. It costs about twenty rupees a day for a bed in hospital. If an operation is involved the anaesthetist charges seven hundred rupees, the surgeon eight hundred rupees and a nurse thirty rupees. Hospital treatment, as you can see, is a luxury which the vast proportion of the population cannot afford. It means too that I cannot send as many patients to hospital as I would like, hence my dream of a hospital of my own where I could put all those who needed specialised treat-ment. This is a difficult task, because the hospitals are scattered over a wide area and public transport can be very trying. Both the Monsoon period and the hot humid pre-Monsoon periods are particularly difficult if you have to move any great distance round the city. Apart from streptomycin, the most used drugs are penicillin and the sulpha drugs for enteritis and dysentery and drugs for asthma and respiratory complaints.

I also have one social worker for six thousand five hundred clients. I believe social workers in the United Kingdom think they are overworked with about eighty clients! She works very hard indeed. Her main task is to go into the slums and *bustee* areas checking on families who have applied to come on the programme. People do not ask just for food cards but for help with all kinds of other things: school fees, clothes, medicine, etc. My social worker is very good at her job. She is, interestingly, a Bengali Muslim who knows her own people and has the uncanny knack of knowing when the complete truth is not being produced. She is known as 'the Muslim with the big Christian heart'.

Stores come from all over the world

Because of the distance involved she uses a jeep. She has to organise her visits well, and usually works by districts except in dire emergencies. She has all the people in the programme listed under districts and manages, somehow, to pay each family a visit every three months. They never know when she is coming; she just arrives at their *bustee* or shack or wherever they are living and sees for herself the condition of the family. She is a very friendly person, very loyal, and we work well together. She has been with me for twelve years now. Perforce, I rely on her a good deal.

Sometimes in the mornings I have to go down to the docks to negotiate the amount of stores coming from foreign countries. The authorities can at times be a bit awkward, but over the years I have discovered that officials normally respond to politeness and courtesy. In the East one learns to cultivate patience and realise that time is not always regarded as the precious commodity it is in the West. I think the dockyard officials find me amusing and try to smooth difficulties for me, because they know that I am not selling the goods that come addressed to me or the Salvation Army, but use them for the good of the poor.

The gates of the Centre open at 12.30 pm and remain open until 2.30 pm, during this time food for three and a half thousand people is distributed. Cooking enough food for them is a major undertaking! Sadly, rice is not provided, because it is rationed in India and because ration cards for such a vast number could not be obtained. The staple

Dishing out

Children await their portion

food is bulghur wheat (an American-prepared grain), lentils and vegetables, selected from egg plants, beans, radishes (which are very popular), carrots, cauliflower, turnips, cucumbers, cabbages and marrow. About five hundred pounds of vegetables are purchased each day at a cost of two hundred rupees. The meal I provide costs the rupee equivalent of about fifteen pence.* Each person receives about two litres of the mixed grain and vegetable. For many this will be the only meal of the day; others, if they are fortunate, may manage to earn a little by minding a baby or washing a car, and can thus afford perhaps a cup of tea and a curry pastry. Depending on generous donations from abroad there are sometimes variations to the diet. To westerners used to eating a variety of food, the food given out daily not only would appear unappetising in the extreme, but also very monotonous. Fortunately, Indians do tend to be ultra-conservative in their diet, eating virtually the same rice meal each day. The average Indian would not thank you for chopping and changing his diet. This, in a way, makes my task easier.

Three thousand five hundred people do not turn up at one time. Women come to collect for the family. Their cards are checked at the gate, and only card-holders are allowed in. I have to be strict about this. Fortunately, as has been said, the Centre is in a side street so the people come and go without much fuss.

I issue the food myself from a large saucepan, and give an amount according

to the number in the family. I have always done this part of the job. I suppose others could do it as well as me, but this is my contact with the people and I like to have personal contact. About five hundred single people actually eat at the Centre. They fill their containers, sit at the table and eat the meal with their fingers in Indian fashion. Many of them are men, some alcoholics, others derelicts; and there are Anglo-Indians, many of them wasters, but without this meal they would perish.

A very sad, but very common problem, is the man who comes to the Centre for a meal—to begin with he is neatly dressed and obviously takes some kind of pride in keeping himself neat and tidy. He informs me he is looking for a job and is confident that his present state of destitution is only a temporary one; he does try very hard to get work. As time goes on his clothes deteriorate and he becomes scruffy. He ceases to wash and shave. He loses what clothes he has. As his pride disappears so his bearing alters, and his manners deteriorate. He is by now sleeping on the pavements and it will take a miracle to rehabilitate him.

The midday queue seems never-ending, but it is always an orderly queue and there is very little talking. They come in, in silence, and those that are eating in the dining room eat in silence. It is almost as if speaking would use up strength which needs to be stored and preserved. I don't speak much either. With some whom I know will respond, I perhaps share a joke, but with the numbers involved, and the size of the waiting queue, I cannot waste time in conversation. I am constantly

* This was the price which obtained in January, 1978.

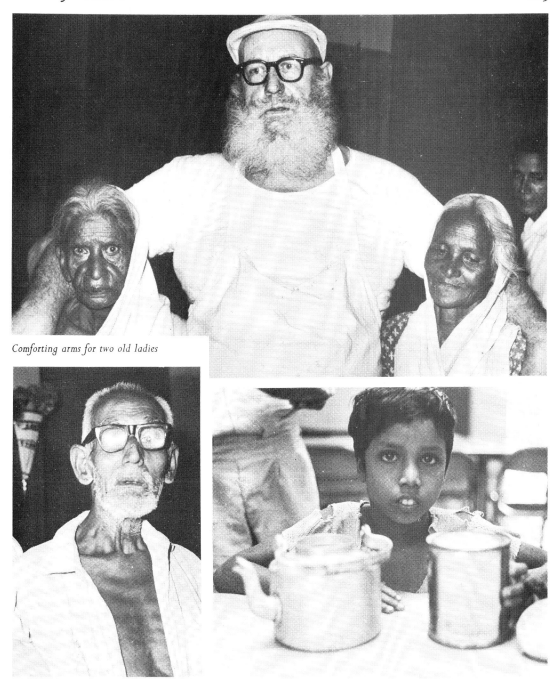

Comforting arms for two old ladies

Old man at the Centre

Boy enjoying a meal at the Centre

DG and hungry customers viewed from inside the food van

touched by the gratitude, which may not always be spoken, but often expressed by the eyes; at times by tears.

Visitors who have witnessed a mealtime in the dining room find it a moving experience, because of the simplicity of the whole proceedings. Feeding, after all, is not something dramatic but something we take for granted. To see this large queue silently filing in, and either leaving with full containers, or sitting down to a meal which tends to be gulped down, rather than savoured and enjoyed, is to see a basic human need gratified. I suppose it is also depressing in the fact that really only one need has been satisfied. Many of them have reached such a low ebb that they have lost their self-respect, and some have adopted the cringing attitude of the professional beggar. There is one very sad Anglo-Indian who boils 'pot' in a dirty container and then injects himself with the same hypodermic needle day after day. His arms are a mass of sores. He spends his life in a daze. I have sent him to Mother Teresa's rehabilitation centre where they try to help him overcome the habit, but eventually he drifts back into the old ways. His life must be a living hell. Is it right to keep him alive? I honestly don't know the answer to that question. It is all very sad and as I stand day by day dishing out food, I am aware that despite the poor image that most of them have of themselves, and the fact that they appear to be the derelicts of society, these are the lucky ones who are at least receiving one hot meal a day, without stealing for it, or without begging for *baksheesh* in the street. I suppose in our

world all things are relative! Amongst the motley crowd are alcoholics, petty thieves, hot-heads, some with small-time jobs, like rag-pickers and paper-pickers, men who scavenge the refuse of the city. I do not object to giving one square meal to these people. The rag-pickers and paper-pickers are at least trying to make a living.

The great number of meals served at this time are not eaten on the spot but are taken away in containers, usually by the mother of the family. Each has a card and on the card the social worker has filled in the number of mouths to feed in the family. From my large saucepan I fill up this container and after all these years I am very accurate at gauging how much to give. The cards, which have been checked at the gate as they come in, are again checked on the way out; so there is really no way that people who have not been vetted can slip through the net. I am quite ruthless about this. As you can imagine, all kinds of spongers attempt to join the queue and slip in. Our regulars, however, have priority. Sometimes if there is some food left over, and there is a poor specimen hanging around the gate, he would be brought in and fed and perhaps even made a regular card holder—if we were convinced that his tale of hardship was true.

There is one old man, for whom I have a tremendous respect. He is seventy years old, and an ex-Salvation Army man and is normally bed-ridden, and we feed him on our evening round of the city. If, however, he is feeling a bit stronger, he literally staggers down to the Centre from his room in Dharamtalla Street. He has not, despite loneliness and ill health, lost his sense of pride.

After washing up the dishes and scrubbing the tables, and hosing down the floor, the first part of the daily operation is over. I am a stickler for cleanliness, and since a great proportion of our clientele are unwashed and many are alive with lice, and many more are suffering from all kinds of diseases, it is imperative that we keep the dining area airy and fresh. Flies in the hot weather are a menace. We have gauze on the windows, but they swarm in through the open door or come in even in the clothes and on the persons of our clients. We wage a constant war against the flies, which unlike many of these humans seem to flourish and grow fat because of the vast amount of uncollected refuse which litters the streets.

Until recently, immediately the lunch was over, we used to start cooking for the clients in the *bustee* areas. These are people who live too far away to use the Centre, or who are too old or sick to make the journey. Some may have small jobs which do not pay enough to maintain a family, such as washing cars or acting as *ayahs*. These jobs can pay as little as twenty rupees per month, and so I augment their rations with one meal a day. Indian families generally eat twice a day only, mornings and evenings, so this service of afternoon food was not fitting properly the eating habits of the people. We therefore changed our round of the outlying *bustee* areas to the evenings, which, as you can appreciate is not so suitable from our point of view in that it

makes for a very long day. However, it does mean that we are doing our nightly tour in the cooler part of the day, so there are compensations. We now cook about 7 pm, and the meal is usually the same as we do for lunch; we load up the three Land Rovers with large containers and each Land Rover covers about eighteen miles of the city. I must say night in Calcutta is more glamorous than the day time. Night draws a curtain over the sores of the city. The lights are bright in the centre of the city, and the neon lights of the night clubs make streets like Park Street seem like any Western city.

But in the outlying *bustee* areas where we go it is different. The street lighting varies from ineffectual to non-existent. There is no glamour there. The stench at night from the open drains is unbelievable, and there is always the trenchant smell of rotting vegetables and coconuts, mingling with other concoctions.

We visit a great number of shut-ins: cripples, old women unable to cope, and the chronically sick; for many of them I am the only visitor of the day. I feel sometimes very guilty that I cannot stay to chat. I know they look forward to my appearing at the door of the hut and, I must say, the blessing which sometimes follows me as I leave, expressed in Bengali, surely one of the most musical of languages, is a source of strength and encouragement to me as I go on my rounds.

The area we cover on this night trip takes in Sealdah, Convent Road, Entally, Chittaranjan Hospital, Park Circus, Ballygunge and across to Dry Dock Area at Kidderpore. I enjoy moving around the city, albeit in rather depressed areas. It is good to get away from the Centre and the smell of cooking and disinfectant, and see the lights and feel part of the vast community which is Calcutta. With the change from the afternoon to evening there is one little luxury I miss. In the middle of the afternoon trip, I used to treat myself to an ice-cream at a very pleasant restaurant in Ballygunge called Quality. I looked forward to sitting and cooling myself in the air-conditioned room and savouring the ice-cream. Now, however, since we do not start until late, we are in a hurry to be finished and so my little indulgence is no more!

Sometimes on the rounds I meet hostility: I have been abused in every Indian dialect there is! I have been spat upon on a number of occasions. I can usually expect trouble when there are political demonstrations going on and, as I said earlier, the Bengali takes his politics very seriously and the odd European who hands out free food can easily become the target for anger and frustration. I often wish my face was a different colour. It would make life much easier if I were Indian. The white man giving out food in a slum area suggests to some of the young hot-heads and radicals white con-descension. Some of the districts are always difficult for me.

I can understand the frustration of the young student. Learning has opened new horizons for him of what society should be like. He learns in the classroom all about democracy and how the power is invested in the people to alleviate social

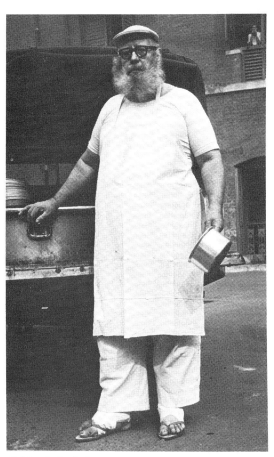

DG beside the food van

Typical street scene in Calcutta. Looking out of the back of the Land Rover with the food tureens brimming with meals on wheels

ills and bring about a brighter to-morrow. He returns from his college to a one-roomed house, which contains about eight people, half of whom are spitting their guts out with tuberculosis. He then sees a white faced man issuing food and knows that this man will return to a clean room, to good food and above all to privacy; his frustration flares up, and I understand this anger and only wish I could help him. This suggests I never get angry. But I do, frequently, and if our positions were reversed I might act the way he does.

The pre-Monsoon period is a most trying time on this evening round. The sun has blazed down all day, the humidity is unbearable and even when one just stands still the perspiration drips off, and even the evenings are hot and clammy. During this period tempers are especially short. People long for the rain to lay the dust and to bring coolness to the atmosphere. The sky during the day is copper and the heat hangs over the city like a blanket. The night-round at this time of the year (April, May and early June) is tiring and sweaty but at the end of it there is the luxury of a bath and dry clothes.

The Monsoon itself brings its own peculiar problems. The torrential rains choke the drains and whole areas are under several feet of water. Despite this, we try our hardest to keep faith with our clients and make every effort to reach our pick-up places. To speed up the operation in various areas we arrange to meet people at central places and when we drive up there is often already a queue formed. This queue sometimes causes difficulties in certain troubled areas. Some trouble-makers want to know why this particular group should be favoured with free food. Some Bengalis who have jobs and earn enough to keep their families are irritated at this group living off charity. One method of showing their displeasure is to beat the side of the Land Rover with their hands. However, from long experience, I know that the secret is not to get riled, not to lose one's temper, to pay no attention to abuse of any kind. I have now the ability to just switch off on occasions where there is trouble. This is the way to survive. If I ever retaliated and perhaps struck an Indian I would be made to suffer in some way, such as the Land Rover being set on fire or overturned. I have to remember at all times I am a guest in India and I hope I always behave with the good manners which are expected of a guest.

I usually return to the Centre about 10 o'clock at night and after cleaning the vehicles and checking the stores in the kitchen, at about 10.30 pm, I climb the stairs rather wearily these days to my room, and shut the door on Calcutta, on the world and its problems. The greatest luxury I enjoy is my evening bath in which I luxuriate for some time. After this I settle down to read or write letters, and enjoy my thoughts and my own company. Although it is at this time that I often regret that I'm not married and have no-one with whom to share the joys and the problems of the day. I never sit idly, as this is when my depression sets in.

I write to some of the one hundred and

String swinger

twenty students I have placed in schools throughout Bengal. These are children from the poorest homes, but who have high IQ's and have the potential, if given the chance, to claw their way out of the slum environment and make good. Indian children are on the whole intelligent children, and Indians in general realise the importance of education. Education means a job, a job means you eat, so there is a respect for school, for the teacher and for someone who can pass on knowledge. If they are considered good material for schooling then I apply for sponsorship from friends abroad and apply to boarding schools for their admission. Boarding schools are essential because the children are taken away from the slum environment where study is really impossible. If you are hungry you don't want to study. If you are oppressed by your environment there is no incentive to study. In some cases too, the parental influence is bad and they are better to be placed in a school in the hills, where they have a chance to make good. They keep contact with their homes of course by letter and in the long winter holidays. The bulk of these children do well. The last time I assessed the reports from the various schools I use, seventy-six per cent of them were doing satisfactorily. This is a very rewarding part of my work. The hope for India lies in the young. My hope and prayer is that the children in my education plan will not suffer the deprivation of their parents, that they will through education escape from the slum environment and the slum mentality.

I find it relatively easy to raise money for sponsorship in foreign countries, sponsors like the personal touch of assisting a child in need and keeping up contacts. So much aid consists of giving money to huge impersonal charities who require vast sums of money to organise and run their affairs. In the Salvation Army's sponsorship scheme all the money given goes to the benefit of the child.

I have always loved children and find I relate easily to them. Indian children with their large liquid eyes and marvellous teeth are most appealing and generally they are intelligent and easily motivated. When I read the school reports from the various hill-schools and mission schools where they have been placed, I feel a real glow to think that I have perhaps been instrumental in giving these girls and boys a chance to prove themselves. One danger, of course, is that this group of children is educated away from their parents. They have been rescued from the slums, but at the cost of the personal relationships with their parents. If they have been educated, say, in a school like the Dr Graham's Homes, Kalimpong, amidst the panoramic sweep of the eternal snows, naturally holiday times are difficult for them when they return to the slum environment. There is the risk that they become ashamed of their parents and the rest of the family. If the home is a bad influence this can be good, but if abject poverty is the only problem of the home, then education and opportunity can be misused. If an unbridgeable gulf is driven between the child and loving parents, I feel about this keenly. It only happens rarely but it does happen from time to time.

Group of students

I write letters to the children I have placed in the schools, letters usually of encouragement and congratulations if they have done well. They often reply, and I, who have never known the joy of fatherhood, of having children of my own, find immense pleasure in receiving letters from my adopted family. They often express gratitude in the uninhibited, flowery language of the Indian. They are not afraid to express emotions like gratitude and even love, and to an old man who lives a hermit-like existence their letters mean a great deal, and this contact with youth keeps me young and is a source of tremendous satisfaction to me.

There is one boy who is my adopted son and who is not only a great help to me in my work but is increasingly becoming my prop in my old age. His name is Michael David and he is now twenty-three years of age. He is a Roman Catholic boy and has a tremendous thirst for knowledge. He has the habit of asking me questions to which I usually don't know the answers! He is an intelligent, honest boy and he takes the place of the son I never had. He takes Monday as his half-day off, and I find Monday the longest day of the week. I miss his chatter and his cheerful presence. He came to me when he was four years old, so our association has stood the test of time. He

is helpful to me in every aspect of the work, and he is definitely one of the bright influences in my life.

I believe that education in the broadest possible sense is India's hope. People must be educated not to produce so many children, they must be educated to be responsible citizens, to have a civic sense, to be hygienic, to keep the streets clean, to use latrines, to take a pride in their homes no matter how humble they are. They must be educated to want to work, to realise that in working there is not only money but satisfaction. Education in India must be more than just learning to read and write, it must be a basic education about living, and values, and having aims and objectives. Education of this nature can counter the terrible apathy and blind acceptance of horrible conditions which is so characteristic of the Calcutta slum-dweller. Gandhi's plans for rural basic education with craft-training at the centre have been largely displaced but, in my humble opinion, they had a great deal of merit. The basic idea was to teach the dignity of labour, and a return to all the simple village crafts which the Mahatma felt were essential to any education programme. I wish I could help hundreds more children to go to good schools, but finance dictates the numbers I can assist.

9 Successes, Failures—and the Future

If one is doing social work of any kind in India, one has to be content with doing a little well. If one becomes obsessed, diverted by the magnitude of the scale of the social problems in India, then one becomes inhibited and depressed and perhaps even broken by the immensity of the problem. Calcutta is no place for the pessimist, the over-sensitive, the person who likes to see quick results. The conditions, the oppressive climate, the disappointments will break such a person's spirit within weeks. I have seen it happen so often. I have seen people come to work here, many of them genuinely feeling that they are responding to God's call to work in the city, and I have seen them depart within the year dispirited, their nerves in such a mess that it will take them some considerable time to recover from the mental and physical battering they have received from Calcutta. Often, too, their faith is shaken as well. No, this is no city for the faint-hearted. It is not just that the fittest of the back street and *bustee* slum-dwellers survive, but also that only the strong amongst those who help them can hope to do so. In my own work, I have a number of successes, but these are balanced by an equal number of failures.

Recently a very neatly dressed man appeared, an Anglo-Indian, and asked me if I recognised him. His face looked vaguely familiar but I could not place him. He informed me that he used to come to the Centre for food until he obtained a job. He had been living on the pavement not far from the Centre; the feeding had tided him over a bad spell. Now he was prosperous. He had his own business, a small car and was grateful for the help which had been given at a time when he needed it. He said that if I ever wanted help just to telephone him as he and his car would always be at my disposal.

An Anglo-Indian man and wife came

for help. He had been a very good engineer, but had become an alcoholic. His wife had struggled to keep the home together but he sold everything for drink. It became obvious that he was incurable and we decided to try to save the wife and children before he dragged them down as well. The social worker managed to find the very capable mother a responsible job as a Matron in a convent in Anansol. The mother now sends money to her husband; he will be permanently on the feeding programme, but his children are receiving a sound education and his wife is happy in her work. It is sad to see a man, who had known good times and who once revelled in his skill and professional ability, destroying himself.

Mohan Biswas was out of work when he came for food. His wife had died and he had two children to support, whom he loved dearly. The social worker placed the children in a country school where they prospered; kind sponsors helped with their school fees. Mohan eventually managed to get a job with the Shipping Corporation of India. He now has his own home, a good secure job, and his children now live at home with him and attend a local school.

Rohit was a small baby in whom I took an interest as I was almost present at his birth; our nurse in fact delivered him. When small and sleeping in a pretty primitive hut with his mother he over-turned a candle, his mother's sari caught fire and she was very severely burned. The poor woman suffered first-degree burns and her leg was badly set in the hospital so that when she recovered she could only crawl. I arranged for her to go into the Calcutta Medical Research Institute where the doctor did a skilful skin-graft and after three months she was able to walk reasonably well. Rohit, who is now fourteen years of age, was put into St Thomas' School, Kidderpore and is doing very well. We helped his mother buy a basket and some fruit and vegetables. Now she walks with a limp but sells enough fruit and vegetables to make about eight rupees a day on which she lives.

A rickshaw-puller came some time ago seeking help. He had no work and he was deeply concerned about his family. I persuaded a local bank to loan him two thousand rupees to purchase a rickshaw. With our help he repays towards this loan each month. His wife has a job as an *ayah* and his children attend a convent school, so fortune has smiled on him.

A great proportion of the men who come don't want food, they want *work*. They often say let me earn my food, let me wash up, clean the vehicles, wipe the tables. Sadly, I cannot have scores of men doing jobs around the place, although I appreciate their sentiments and respect them for thinking that way. Naturally, there are others who are quite happy to accept the food and are not interested in finding work. Employment I know is difficult in western countries at the moment; here in India with so many without education and without luck, employment is impossible. They have nothing to offer a prospective employer, and for labouring, unskilled jobs they are so physically weak through malnutrition

Salvation Army officers and DG hear the tale of man who has been assisted

that they are not fit even for the most menial tasks.

One of my greatest success stories concerns a man who is now a supervisor in the docks and is doing splendidly. When I see him, I find it difficult to remember him as the same person who was once on my feeding programme. These successes keep me going in more depressing times.

To balance these success stories are many disappointments. Some of our seed falls on stony ground. Some appear to make good and obtain jobs, and then alcohol or just sheer stupidity or laziness or dishonesty, brings them back to the gate pleading for a meal as they are yet again destitute. Christ's story of the shepherd concerning himself over the one sheep out of the hundred has often been a comfort to me. Very often I have to be content with limited success, but I cheer myself when I realise that without the one meal a day many of the six thousand would not survive, or if they did survive they would do so by stealing.

I am often asked about the attitude of the Indian Government or, rather, the West Bengal Government to my work. I have had no interference of any description, and there has been no official comment ever made to me from Government sources. Queen Elizabeth recognised my work with the award of the MBE, in 1974. I was pleased about this and received the award here in my kitchen. I receive no Government aid for my work and I do not ask for it. I think the West Bengal Government have enough

Fittingly, Major Dudley Gardiner received MBE award in his own kitchen from the High Commissioner, Sir Terence Garvie (1974)

problems of their own without worrying about me.

The problems of the West Bengal Government are not simply confined to the boundaries of the city of Calcutta. There are vast problems of poverty and deprivation in the hinterland as well. Calcutta has not a monopoly of misery and slum conditions, although in urban areas the problems are more intensified. Living in Calcutta, one tends to forget that India is really a land of villages. Out in the country, however, the social problems are not so pronounced. The villagers live simply and regulate their simple lives according to the cycle of nature. Urban deprivation is more dramatic and more depressing.

I am often asked if I will retire. My health has been pretty ropey recently but I continue despite considerable physical discomfort. *I cannot retire.* Too many people depend on me. I personally do not think I would survive retirement for very long. I made a promise when I started this feeding programme that I would do thirty-six years. I have sixteen more years to go! I hope to die in harness. Sadly, I think the feeding programme will die with me. I do not honestly think anyone will take the job on after I die. I do not think anyone would be prepared to work sixteen hours a day, seven days a week, every day of the year. I do not say that with pride; I am simply being realistic. People have families, responsibilities, desire for holidays and days off which are very natural. I am the unnatural case in having lived such an eccentric life for the past twenty years. It would be difficult to find someone with the same mentality as me. Please do not think I regard myself as a glorious martyr, serving suffering humanity at vast cost to myself. I enjoy my work. It suits me. I am now conditioned to my anti-social job. Like the hermit, I like the quality of my life, just as presumably monks and nuns do when they enter strict religious orders. I feel fulfilled in my job.

The ideal solution would be if I could find an Indian to be my heir. I have to say that I think this is unlikely. The Indian mentality is not suited to this type of work. The ascetic Hindu *sadhu* can bear deprivation and physical discomfort, but it is the sheer consistency which the job demands which makes me unsure if an Indian could cope with it. I may be being rather boastful and even pig-headed when I claim that no-one could take over from me. Of course, I would be delighted to be proved wrong. No-one is indispensable and it may be that one day someone will wander into the Centre here and offer his services, and he might well be prepared to learn what it is all about and be prepared to take on the responsibility of my extended family. Nothing would give me greater pleasure.

I hope I have done my little bit to help India. I love India with a passion which is profound. It is unpredictable, India has as many moods as a capricious woman, but India is never dull, never ordinary. I love the illogicalities, the striking contrasts, the movement, the colour. India is like a picture painted in blazing oils, it is compulsive and strains the emotions to the limits. I shall be happy to die here in my adopted country, and I hope that I will be remembered perhaps as someone who tried to do his bit to help a few of the unfortunates of this city.

I hope when my time comes to shuffle off this mortal coil, I will have the same deep faith and love as did Bengal's favourite son, Rabindranath Tagore who, when nearing death wrote:

'A summons has come and I am ready for my journey. At this time of my parting wish me good luck my friends. The sky is flushed with the dawn and my path lies beautiful. I shall put on my wedding garland. The evening star will come out when my voyage is done and the plaintive notes of the twilight melodies be struck from the King's gateway'.

Hindu sadhu

Index

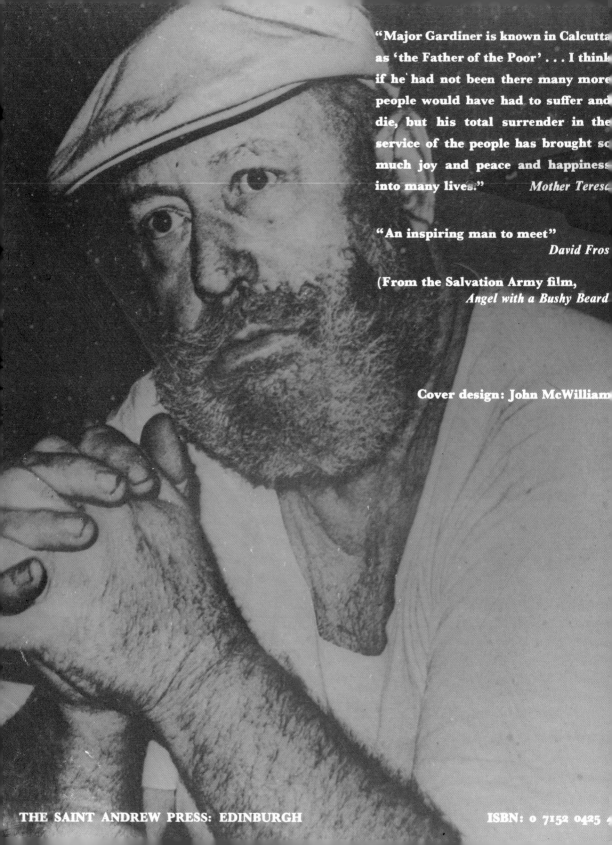

"Major Gardiner is known in Calcutta
as 'the Father of the Poor' . . . I think
if he had not been there many more
people would have had to suffer and
die, but his total surrender in the
service of the people has brought so
much joy and peace and happiness
into many lives." *Mother Teresa*

"An inspiring man to meet"
David Frost

(From the Salvation Army film,
Angel with a Bushy Beard

Cover design: John McWilliam

THE SAINT ANDREW PRESS: EDINBURGH   ISBN: 0 7152 0425